THE RETIREMENT FREEDOM GUIDE

DAVID TIDWELL
CHAD NIELSEN

This book discusses general concepts for retirement planning, and is not intended to provide tax or legal advice. Individuals are urged to consult with their tax and legal professionals regarding these issues. It is important to know a) that annuities and some of their features have costs associated with them; b) that annuities used to fund IRAs do not afford any additional measure of tax deferral for the IRA owner; c) that income received from annuities and securities may be taxable; and d) that securities' past performance does not influence or predict future results.

Copyright © 2016 by Gradient Positioning Systems, LLC. All rights reserved. No part of this publication may be reproduced, distributed, or transmitted in any form or by any means, electronic or mechanical, including photocopying, recording, or by any information storage and retrieval system, without written permission of the publisher, except in the case of brief quotations embodied in critical reviews and certain other noncommercial uses permitted by copyright law.

Printed in the United States of America

First Printing, 2016

Gradient Positioning Systems, LLC
4105 Lexington Avenue North, Suite 110
Arden Hills, MN 55126
(877) 901-0894

Contributors: Nick Stovall, Mike Binger, Nate Lucius and Gradient Positioning Systems, LLC.

Gradient Positioning Systems, LLC, Chad Nielsen, and David Tidwell are not affiliated with or endorsed by the Social Security Administration or any government agency.

TABLE OF CONTENTS

10 KEY QUESTIONS TO ANSWER BEFORE RETIREMENT..........1

CHAPTER 1: YOUR IDEAL RETIREMENT..........11

CHAPTER 2: AN EXAMINATION OF RISK..........29

CHAPTER 3: REVIEWING YOUR INCOME NEEDS..........39

CHAPTER 4: STRATEGIES FOR FEDERAL EMPLOYEES..........47

CHAPTER 5: UNDERSTANDING SOCIAL SECURITY..........77

CHAPTER 6: FILLING YOUR INCOME GAP..........93

CHAPTER 7: THE IMPACT OF MARKET VOLATILITY..........107

CHAPTER 8: WHY YOU SHOULD CONSIDER MANAGED MONEY..........115

CHAPTER 9: NEW IDEAS FOR INVESTING..........131

CHAPTER 10: BE PREPARED FOR TAXES..........137

CHAPTER 11: THE FUTURE OF U.S. TAXATION..........149

CHAPTER 12: THE BRANDEIS STORY..........167

CHAPTER 13: YOUR LEGACY BEYOND DOLLARS AND CENTS..........175

CHAPTER 14: HOW TO AVOID THE BIG LEGACY MISTAKES..........183

CHAPTER 15: CHOOSING A QUALIFIED RETIREMENT PRO..........197

GLOSSARY..........215

10 KEY QUESTIONS
TO ANSWER BEFORE RETIREMENT

"Those who fail to plan, plan to fail."
— Benjamin Franklin

For individuals retiring today, the most common question isn't *"when can I retire,"* but rather, *"can I afford to retire?"* We live in a very different retirement world now than we did just 15 years ago. Even though you have worked hard, prepared and started early, you might be entering into a time without a paycheck that could potentially last longer than your time of employment. A look back at graphs illustrating the behavior of our financial markets over the last 15 years reveals that major market swings are happening much closer together now, and many low-risk vehicles such as those used by our grandparents aren't breaking even with inflation. It seems today's investors are forced to choose to either go broke safely or risk seeing as much as 50 percent of their portfolios erased from the books. These options don't exactly inspire confidence when it comes to the task of creating steady income or leaving a legacy. Thankfully, there are better alternatives. Finding the best alternatives is what this book is all about.

Before you take that leap off the retirement cliff, take the time now to answer the following 10 questions. Doing so can help this transition feel less like a free-fall and more like a series of simple, practical steps.

QUESTION #1: HOW MUCH WILL MY PENSION BE?

It used to be that employees were rewarded for their hard work and loyalty with **defined-benefit pension plans,** which meant that when they retired they could expect a known (defined) benefit amount most of us call a pension.

The Federal **Civil Service Retirement System** (CSRS) established in 1920 is a defined-benefit pension plan and provides qualifying federal workers a substantial amount of retirement income. How much will that pension amount be? The amount depends on a variety of factors, which we will address in Chapter 4, *Strategies for Federal Employees.*

More and more, however, today's workers are in charge of designing their own pension plans. Traditional defined-benefit plans are being replaced with **defined-contribution plans.** These plans put the burden of saving (contribution) on your shoulders, and they function more as one leg of a three-legged retirement income stool. For Federal employees, the newer **Federal Employees Retirement System** (FERS) enacted in 1983 operates assuming these three distinct components: Social Security benefits, a defined-contribution plan, and a defined-benefit plan (or pension) not designed to be the sole source of your income. Getting all three legs of the retirement income stool to work together gets difficult once it comes time to retire, which is why you need a comprehensive plan.

FERS employees will need to go through the same process we recommend every retiree go through: a comprehensive analysis of their income producing benefits. This is done to assure you end up with the maximum amount of income. Chapters 1, 2 and 3 take you through this process. Once you have an understanding of your current position, Chapter 6, *Filling the Income Gap,* shows you how to convert a portion of your savings into a pension-like benefit that offers more flexibility than traditional pensions using one of the most potent investment tools available today: the income annuity.

Although a lot of negative media attention has been centered on annuities, the word **annuity** simply means the annual payment of income. By creating your own pension annuity, you can effectively secure yourself a regular paycheck during retirement that is customized to fit your exact expense needs.

QUESTION #2: WHAT PENSION SURVIVOR OPTIONS SHOULD I CHOOSE?

Even if you won't be receiving a pension, survivorship planning is a crucial component of your plan and an area often overlooked. For married couples, when one spouse dies, there will be one less Social Security check and in many cases, the loss or reduction of a pension. How will that affect the surviving spouse's ability to pay the bills? Planning for spousal continuation is covered in Chapter 3, *Reviewing Your Income Needs.*

For military and federal employees, or anyone who has a defined pension benefit, the election of your pension benefits is one of the biggest decisions you will make. Your particular death benefits are based on what's known as your *Survivorship Options.* As part of a comprehensive planning process, we will walk you through a process we call **Pension Maximization** in Chapter 4.

QUESTION #3: WHAT SHOULD I DO WITH MY RETIREMENT SAVINGS?

This question speaks to all high-risk qualified retirement plans funded with pre-tax dollars including the following accounts:
- IRA
- 401(k)
- TSP
- 403(b)
- Deferred compensation plan
- SEP and Simple IRA
- Profit sharing plans
- Stock option plans

One of the biggest concerns and problems with defined-contribution plans is what to do with the money at retirement. With the old defined-benefit plans, you didn't have to go to the trouble of making these major financial decisions. Ignoring this stage of the process today, however, can lead to major financial suffering. This was recently evidenced by the retirees who lost 40 percent or more of their portfolios during the Great Recession of 2008. Chapter 2, *An Examination of Risk,* walks you through a process to help you structure this money by addressing the following three questions:
- How much should I structure for income?
- How much should I keep liquid?
- How much should I invest for growth?

This is one area more than any other where you really need the experience and guidance of a financial professional who has a vested interest in your well-being.

QUESTION #4: HOW WILL I FILL MY RETIREMENT INCOME GAP?

The difference between the amount of money you know you have from guaranteed sources of income (such as your Social Security and defined-pension benefits) and the amount of money you need to meet your ongoing expenses is known as the Income Gap. How you structure your retirement assets to fill this gap affects the quality of your lifestyle, your ability to prepare for the potential of long-term care and the legacy you will leave for your family. Chapter 7, *The Impact of Market Volatility*, warns against relying on the stock market as the primary basis for filling your income gap.

QUESTION #5: SHOULD I CONSIDER USING AN IRA?

One way to structure the money from your TSP or 401(k) savings plan is inside of an IRA. There may be some tax-related advantages to moving your money into an IRA. IRAs offer more favorable distribution options and more flexible investment opportunities. Chapter 4 lists these advantages and explains why this can be such a helpful strategy for federal employees. Chapter 10, *Be Prepared for Taxes*, walks you through what you need to be aware of as you start spending the money in your tax-qualified saving plans.

QUESTION #6: IS MY CURRENT LIFE INSURANCE PLAN RIGHT FOR MY FAMILY DURING RETIREMENT?

We find that many people enter into retirement without the life insurance coverage they think they have, or with coverage they don't even need. With its ability to provide tax-free benefits to your spouse and loved ones, life insurance can be a big part of the retirement planning process. Federal employees who have a Federal Employee Group Life Insurance plan (FEGLI) need to realize the limitations and expense of their coverage, and married couples may want to consider life insurance as part of their long-term financial plan. You might also say that anybody who loves somebody should have life insurance, which is why Chapter 14, *How To Avoid the Big Legacy Mistakes*, is devoted to this valuable legacy tool.

QUESTION #7: WHEN IS THE BEST TIME TO START MY SOCIAL SECURITY BENEFIT?

Although Social Security can seem like a relatively straightforward decision, figuring out when and how to file as well as how this income affects your taxes and other benefits can quickly become an overwhelming process. Chapter 4, *Understanding Social Security*, takes you through an education process and teaches you what you need to know before claiming this important lifelong benefit. Federal employees in the FERS retirement system, who are eligible for Social Security benefits and who retire before age 62 can also receive supplemental benefits not available to the general public, which is one reason why you want to be aware of the filing strategies discussed in Chapter 4.

QUESTION #8: SHOULD I GET MEDICARE PART A AND PART B?

Medicare is an earned benefit you have been paying into during your working years so that once you reach age 65 you can receive guaranteed health benefits. Generally speaking, Medicare is broken into four parts labeled by the letters A, B, C and D.

- Medicare Part A offers a hospitalization benefit that covers most medically necessary hospital stays, skilled nursing facilities, home health and hospice care for a maximum period of 90 days. It is not designed for long-term stays but rather is designed for patients during recovery.
- Medicare Part B functions like a basic health insurance plan and covers medically necessary doctor services, preventive care, durable medical equipment, hospital

outpatient services, laboratory tests, x-rays, mental health care, and some home health and ambulance services.
- Medicare Part C allows private health insurance companies to provide supplemental Medicare benefits.
- Medicare Part D provides outpatient prescription drug benefits.*

We've found that most Federal employees receive really good health care benefits and so they choose to keep those benefits. With the comprehensive benefits offered by plans such as Tri-Care, they don't need to take on the expense of paying an additional premium to double their coverage. This influences pension election decisions, particularly for married couples, which is why these strategies are discussed further in Chapter 4.

QUESTION #9: WHAT IS MY PLAN TO PAY FOR LONG-TERM CARE?

As life expectancies increase, incorporating an element of long-term care planning is vital to the stability of every retirement plan. There are several strategies to use when preparing for this type of unforeseen event, including newer strategies that offer an improvement to the traditional use-it-or-lose-it solutions. These strategies are discussed as part of our comprehensive risk analysis done in Chapter 2.

QUESTION #10: ARE MY BENEFICIARY DESIGNATIONS UPDATED AND CORRECT?

This last question is a critical determinant to the overall success of your plan. One of the biggest estate planning errors we see is a relatively simple matter to correct. Beneficiary designations

---

* *http://www.medicareinteractive.org/page2.php?topic=counselor&page=script&script_id=214*

supersede what you put in your will or trust because they are contractual payouts. Chapter 13, *Your Legacy Beyond Dollars And Cents*, gives you a list of legal documents you will want to review to make sure your legacy plan fits with your intentions.

ABOUT US

We are Chad Nielsen and David Tidwell, colleagues and financial professionals who are trained federal benefits consultants living in the state of Idaho. **While we each have our own separate firms in different cities, we share a common objective:** *a desire to help educate people at or nearing retirement about the importance of making correct financial decisions.* Many of these decisions are final, yet they go on to affect the quality of life for you and your loved ones for years to come. During our 52 years of combined industry experience, we have seen time and again how doing the wrong thing with your money can severely impact your ability to enjoy the freedom of a successful retirement. For these reasons, we have put our heads together to write a retirement planning book that specifically addresses the challenges faced by retirees today.

The book is organized so anyone retiring with a nest egg of assets can benefit from the knowledge and advice, but we also took the time to address issues specific to federal employees. We have found information regarding retirement for federal employees difficult to assimilate and hard to interpret. Retirement is one game in life you can't afford to lose. It is our aim to provide a sound formula you can use to secure the winning retirement you would like.

TWO FIRMS, ONE PHILOSOPHY

We come from similar backgrounds, and share a philosophy taught to us by our ancestors. It reminds us that the older we get, the harder we want our money to work for us. We were taught that *during retirement, you want to be able to make money while you sleep.* Whether you are receiving a pension check or payouts from an interest-earning investment, you deserve the freedom and peace of mind that comes from knowing the money will be there.

When you work with us to get an income plan in place, you don't have to worry about what the market is doing from day-to-day, and you don't have to worry about managing your money. Our strategies are designed to help you improve your position and maximize your benefits. By making the best choices today, you will be positioned for the best possible future tomorrow. The questions you are considering now can all be answered. The answers for each person will be different depending on your individual situation. The ensuing chapters of this book can give you a more confident approach to retirement by giving you the knowledge you need to address your financial situation from four different perspectives:

- Income
- Asset accumulation
- Taxes
- Legacy

While most professionals in the financial services industry are focused on helping people "save enough", our goal is to help people understand how to best manage their savings and the various risks so they can have enough income to achieve financial peace and security. This is a different way of thinking, and it requires a different type of advisor. We are that type of advisors. We are certified in Federal Government Benefits and familiar with the challenges unique to people retiring from federal service and other careers. As independent Investment Advisor Representatives (IARs), we are also held to the highest standards in the industry. We have complete access to the investments, tools and strategies you need to successfully retire in today's economy.

Retirement is a time of many decisions, options and choices. It can also be the most exciting and freeing time of your life. We invite you to work with us and invest in your future so you can have the confidence to pursue the retirement you've always envisioned.

– *Chad Nielsen*, Investment Advisor Representative, Trained Federal Benefit Consultant and President of Gateway Financial and Estate Planning, Inc.

– *David Tidwell*, Investment Advisor Representative, Retirement Planning Specialist, Trained Federal Benefits Consultant, President of Legacy Financial Advisors, Inc. & Interwest Investment Advisors Inc.

1
YOUR IDEAL RETIREMENT

A good retirement is more than just money.

Will your pension benefit, Social Security benefit, and other retirement savings be enough? If you're like Dave and Lori, you hope so. When the couple turned 60 years old, they started thinking about what their lives would be like in the next 10 years. When would they retire? What would their retirement look like? How much money did they have and what should they do with it?

Dave has a modest pension that he can begin collecting at age 62, but as a Federal employee, he doesn't know which survivorship options he should choose. Although he is eligible to retire early, he doesn't know if they can realistically afford it.

Lori has an IRA she's been contributing to and she has her Social Security benefit, but she doesn't know if she can count on either of *them to fund her retirement. She has seen how public policy changes have reduced benefits that were promised to retirees. During the last 15 years, she has seen the value of her IRA fluctuate dramatically due to market volatility. Where is the best place to put this money, and how can she turn it into a pension that will give her a monthly income?*

While Dave and Lori may sound like they're totally in the dark about their retirement, the truth is there are a lot of people just like them. They know retirement is coming and know they have some assets to rely on, but they aren't sure how it will all come together to provide them with a retirement income.

You spend your entire working life hoping what you put into your retirement accounts will help you live comfortably once you clock out of the workforce for good. The key word in that sentiment and the word that can make retirement feel like a looming problem instead of a rewarding life stage, is ***hope***. You hope you'll have enough money.

Expectations about what retirement is and what people *hope* it will look like have changed dramatically over the years. Our grandparents who retired hoped to go on a cruise or maybe one big trip before settling down to enjoy their golden years at home. The life expectancy at birth back in 1930 was age 58 for men and age 62 for women, which meant most people felt lucky to even reach retirement.*

Today's retirement expectations have gone up right along with life expectancy rates. According to the 2011 Social Security actuaries table, the average 65-year-old male today can expect to live another 17.6 years; the average 65-year old woman another 20 years.** Not only can today's retirees expect to make it to age 65,

---

* *https://www.ssa.gov/history/lifeexpect.html*
** *https://www.ssa.gov/oact/STATS/table4c6.html*

but they'll still be going strong. With that comes the desire to do more things than ever. People are starting businesses, new hobbies, volunteering and taking on causes important to them. With more and more families spread out across the country, many retirees are spending more money on travel, nicer cars, nicer homes and spiffy-looking RVs.

While all of this costs money, a good retirement is about more than just having money; it's about your ability to do what you want to be doing. Whether or not those activities cost money is just part of the planning equation.

The first step when determining whether or not you'll have enough money to retire is to identify what it is you expect your retirement to look like. Leaving your retirement up to chance is unadvisable by nearly any standard, yet millions of people find themselves *hoping* instead of planning for a happy ending. By taking the time now to identify what you want, you can put a plan together that gives you the confidence of *knowing* you can achieve your ideal.

WHERE ARE YOU GOING?

Money represents more than the paper it's printed on. It is the embodiment of your time, your talents, and your commitments. It buys the food you eat, the house you sleep in, the car you drive, and the clothes you wear. It also helps provide you with the lifestyle you want to live once you retire.

You have spent a lifetime earning it, spending it, and hopefully, accumulating it. When the time comes for retirement, you want your money to provide you with a comfortable lifestyle and stable income after your working days are done. You might also have other desires, such as traveling, purchasing property, or moving to be closer to your family (or farther away). You may also want your assets to provide for your loved ones after you are gone.

The truth is that it takes more than just money to fulfill those needs and desires. Your income, your plans for retirement, your future healthcare expenses, and the continued accumulation of your assets after you stop working and drawing a paycheck all rely on one thing: *You.*

The best retirements aren't going *from* something but *to* something. Now that you are finally able to quit doing what you *have* to do to make a living, you have an opportunity to do what you *want* to do to make a life. What are those things? What makes you feel good and happy and fulfilled? What is your plan for retirement?

It's amazing how few people have really given these questions much thought. Today's workers have a lot of fear concerning their retirement years, especially federal employees who are often retiring at a much younger age. After spending a lifetime centered on work, family and career, it's sometimes difficult to switch gears and think about life outside of a job.

On the other hand, we've also been amazed at the wide variety of things people decide they want to do with their retirement years once they sit down and give it some real thought. We've seen everything from moving to Mexico to live like royalty, doing missionary work to raising grandkids, and even traveling around the world sewing quilts. One thing is clear*: **the ones who are the most certain about their retirement and feel the most confident are the people who have taken the time to identify what they are going to do.*** If spending time in nature examining wildlife is what makes you feel the most fulfilled, then you're not going to need as much money as someone who wants to travel the world, staying in five-star hotels and eating in restaurants. What your retirement will look like is ultimately up to you.

WHAT YOU ARE SHOOTING FOR: 6 RETIREMENT GOALS TO ACHIEVE YOUR IDEAL

Once you identify what you want to do when you get to retirement, the next step is to identify what you have to work with to help you get there. While it's true that the money you have to work with is often over-emphasized, it does make up a big part of the retirement equation. To secure your ideal retirement, you'll want to examine the following six areas of financial concern:

A monthly base retirement income: Generally speaking, you'll want to look at replacing from 90 to 100 percent of your employment NET income. We specify net income here because for most people, this is what you are used to living on. For most federal employees in particular, the difference between your take-home pay and your top-line salary is anywhere from 40 to 50 percent. How much of your income is actually coming home? That is the target number we want to look at replacing.

All debts paid off: Cash flow during retirement is very important. We advocate for no debt during retirement, because those monthly payments and interest charges can drain your income. Often the question is brought up: *What about the tax advantage of having mortgage interest?* While every situation is different and you will want to have a professional examine yours, we generally find that people find themselves in a lower tax bracket during retirement. Once there, your tax burden is minimal, and it no longer makes sense to spend a dollar (of interest) in order to save a dime (of taxes), so to speak. But the main objective is to minimize or eliminate taking money from your income to service debt.

A potential source of additional income for later years: Many people underestimate how inflation can erode your purchasing power. We talked earlier about today's life expectancy rates: most of us can expect to need at least 20 years if not more of retirement income. When you consider that in the United States, a gallon of regular gas cost $1.11 in 1990 and then $3.36 in 2014, you'll understand why everybody wants to secure a pay raise at least once during retirement.*

Liquid assets available for emergencies and opportunities: A liquid asset is one that you can access as actual cash for easy spending. A certain amount of liquidity is necessary during retirement because you want to be able to access your money quickly and easily when unexpected expenses or opportunities crop up. These expenses can be good, such as an opportunity to go on a cruise with your children, or they can be those emergency expenses like needing new tires for the RV. Whatever the case may be, we recommend building an emergency fund of three to six months in savings or money market accounts.

Investments for long-term growth: After the emergency fund has been established, you'll want to put together an accumulation plan for longer-term growth funds. In addition to the immediate access funds, you'll also want a medium term fund set for an intermediate period of growth, say five years, and a long-term fund set for 10 years or longer. When you can set aside money that you know you won't have to access for longer periods, you have more opportunity for growth.

A good plan: Without a good plan in place, you have no way of knowing how much money you need for your income and how much you can set aside for growth, which means you have no way to reduce or eliminate the amount of risk your retirement savings are exposed to. The key to figuring out how much income you'll need all starts with identifying what your ideal retirement looks like.

---

* http://www.statista.com/statistics/204740/retail-price-of-gasoline-in-the-united-states-since-1990/

- How will you use your new free time?
- What personal and family goals do you hope to accomplish?
- What great things have you always wanted to do, but never had the time?

Now is your chance to answer these questions. Doing so will allow you to turn the fear of "hope so" around in to a retirement based on "know so" and designed to achieve your ideal.

GETTING THERE VS. STAYING THERE

Saving and investing for retirement is what we call "Getting There". Many people have developed a fairly large nest egg during their working years. You could say they have "arrived" at a place of financial security. The problem is that the financial industry and most advisors have a tunnel vision focus on accumulating large retirement funds with almost no thought as to what to do with all these savings. The giant question at retirement becomes what is the right way of using this hard earned savings to create security for a lifetime? We call this crucial planning "Staying There", or maintaining financial security.

The investment strategies that you used ***getting to retirement*** are often very different from the ones you need to use to ***stay there***. From an investment perspective, retirement strategies are often a mirror image of accumulation strategies. Setting up a flawed strategy could put you in a positon to endure every retiree's worst fear: ***running out of money.***

It works like this:
- To get to your retirement years, you focus on working, saving and accumulating money. You receive regular paychecks, and your nest egg receives regular replenishment. These are known as *the accumulation years*. The investment

strategies you used for accumulation (dollar cost averaging, for example) are what got you here.
- To stay in retirement without having to go back to work, adjust your expectations or lower your quality of life, it is important to shift your paradigm from the accumulation phase to *the distribution phase*. It's a lot like arriving at a fort. Once there, the first thing you want to do is to protect yourself against invasions of market volatility, inflation and long-term care. This process, financially speaking, is like fortifying your walls and can be thought of as *the preservation stage*: you will take stock of your supplies and protect what you can before you start going out and spending that money.

Many investors struggle with this realization. They remain stuck in growth-mode because they have been responsible for the growth and accumulation of assets that got them here. The problem is that staying stuck in growth mode and relying on growth-only strategies poses a real threat to today's retirees who rely more and more on defined-contribution benefits. These plans don't automatically generate a pension substantial enough for most people to live on. They also don't protect you from the attacks to your savings that happen during the epic of today's retirements.

So many people fail to make this distinction that economist Robert C. Merton refers to it as, "*The Crisis in Retirement Planning*" in his 2014 article for the Harvard Business Review:

"Investment decisions are now focused on the value of the funds, the returns on investment they deliver, and how volatile those returns are. Yet the primary concern of the saver remains what it always has been: Will I have sufficient income in retirement to live comfortably?"

The reality is that investment strategies and savings plans that worked in the past have encountered challenging new circumstances that have turned them on their heads. The Great Recession of the early 2000's highlighted how old investment ideas were not only ineffective but incredibly destructive to the retirement plans of millions of Americans. The dawn of an entirely restructured health care system brings with it new options and challenges that will undoubtedly change the way insurance companies provide investment products and services.

Perhaps the most important lessons investors learned from the Great Recession is that not understanding where your money is invested (and the potential risks of those investments) can work against you, your plans for retirement and your legacy. Saving and investing money isn't enough to truly get the most out of it. You must have a well-planned approach to managing your assets.

HOPE SO VS. KNOW SO MONEY

Essentially, managing your money and your investments is an ongoing process that requires customization and adaptation to a changing world. And make no mistake; the world is always changing. What worked for your parents or even your parents' parents was probably good advice back then. People in retirement or approaching retirement today need new ideas and professional guidance. Let's take a look at some of the basic truths about money as it relates to saving for retirement.

There are essentially two kinds of money: *Hope So* and *Know So*. Everyone can divide their money into these two categories. Some have more of one kind than the other. The goal isn't to eliminate one kind of money but to balance them as you approach retirement.

Hope So Money is money that is at risk. It fluctuates with the market. It has no minimum guarantee. It is subject to investor activity, stock prices, market trends, buying trends, etc. You get the picture. This money is exposed to more risk but also has the potential for more reward. Because the market is subject to change, you can't really be sure what the value of your investments will be worth in the future. You can't really *rely* on it at all. For this reason, we refer to it as Hope So Money. This doesn't mean you shouldn't have some money invested in the market, but it would be dangerous to assume you can know what it will be worth in the future.

Hope So Money is an important element of a retirement plan, especially in the early stages of planning when you can trade volatility for potential returns, and when a longer investment timeframe is available to you. In the long run, time can smooth out the ups and downs of money exposed to the market. Working with a professional and leveraging a long-term investment

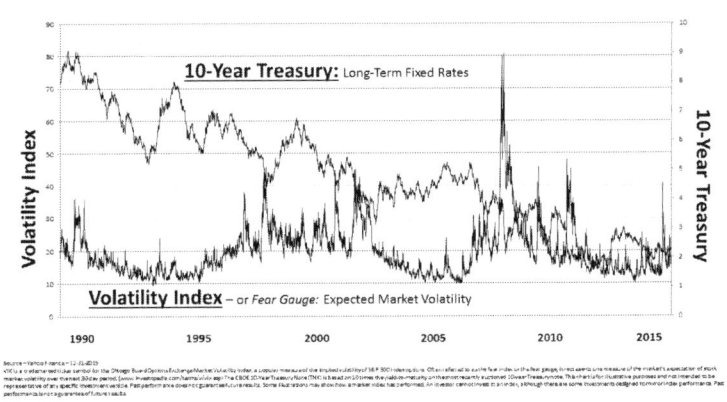

The VIX, or volatility index, of the market represents expected market volatility. When the VIX Drops, economic experts expect less volatility. When the VIX rises, more volatility is expected.

1. *VIX is a trademarked ticker symbol for the Chicago Board Options Exchange (CBOE) Market Volatility Index, a popular measure of the implied volatility of S&P 500 index options. Often referred to as the fear index or the fear gauge, it represents one measure of the market's expectation of stock market volatility over the next 30 day period. (wikipedia.com)*
2. *The CBOE 10-Year Treasury note (TNX) is based on 10 times the yield-to-maturity on the most recently auctioned 10-year Treasury note.*

strategy has the potential to create rewarding returns from Hope So Money.

Know So Money, on the other hand, is safer when compared to Hope So Money. Know So Money is made up of dependable, low-risk or no-risk money, and investments that you can count on. Social Security is one of the most common forms of Know So Money. Income you draw or will draw from Social Security is guaranteed. You have paid into Social Security your entire career, and you can rely on that money during your retirement. Unlike the market, rates of growth for Know So Money are dependent on 10-year treasury rates. The 10-year treasury, or TNX, is commonly considered to represent a very secure and safe place for your money, hence Know So Money. The 10-year treasury drives key rates for things such as mortgage rates or CD rates. Know So Money may not be as exciting as Hope So Money, but it is safer. You can safely be fairly sure you will have it in the future.

Knowing the difference between Hope So and Know So Money is an important step towards a successful retirement plan. People who are 55 or older and who are looking ahead to retirement should be relying on more Know So Money than Hope So Money.

Ideally, the rates of return on Hope So and Know So Money would have an overlapping area that provided an acceptable rate of risk for both types of money. In the early 1990s, interest rates were high and market volatility was low. At that time, you could invest in either Hope So or Know So Money options because the rates of return were similar from both Know So and Hope So investments, and you were likely to be fairly successful with a wide range of investment options. At that time, you could expose yourself to an acceptable amount of risk or an acceptable fixed rate. Basically, it was difficult to make a mistake during that time period. Today, you don't have those options. Market volatility is at all-time highs while interest rates are at all-time lows. They are so far apart from each other that it is hard to know what to do with your money.

Yesterday's investment rules may not work today. Not only could they hamper achieving your goals, they may actually harm your financial situation. We are currently in a period when the rates for Know So Money options are at historic lows, and the volatility of Hope So Money is higher than ever. There is no overlapping acceptable rate, making both options less than ideal. *Because of this uncertain financial landscape, wise investment strategies are more important now than ever.*

This unique situation requires fresh ideas and investment tools that haven't been relied on in the past. Investing the way your parents did will not pay off. The majority of investment ideas used by financial professionals in the 1990s aren't applicable to today's markets. That kind of investing will likely get you in trouble and compromise your retirement. Today, you need a better PLAN.

HOW MUCH RISK ARE YOU EXPOSED TO?

Many investors don't know how much risk they are exposed to. It is helpful to organize your assets so you can have a clear understanding of how much of your money is at risk and how much is in safer holdings. This process starts with listing all your assets.

Let's take a look at the two kinds of money:

Hope So Money is, as the name indicates, money that you *hope* will be there when you need it. Hope So Money represents what you would like to get out of your investments. Examples of Hope So Money include:
- Stock market funds, including index funds
- Mutual funds
- Variable annuities
- REITS

Know So Money is money that you know you can count on. It is safer money that isn't exposed to the level of volatility as the asset types noted above. You can more confidently count on having this money when you need it. Examples of Know So Money are:
- Government backed bonds
- Savings and checking accounts
- Fixed income annuities
- CDs
- Treasuries
- Money market accounts

> » *Mark had a modest brokerage account that he added to when he could. When he changed jobs a couple years ago, at age 58, Mark transferred his 401(k) assets into an IRA. Just a few years from retirement, he is now beginning to realize that nearly every dollar he has saved for retirement is subject to market risk.*
>
> *Intuitively, he knows that the time has come to shift some assets to an alternative that is safer, but how much is the right amount?*

UNDERSTANDING THE RULE OF 100

Determining the amount of risk that is right for you is dependent on a number of variables. You need to feel comfortable with where and how you are investing your money, and your financial professional is obligated to help you make decisions that put your money in places that fit your risk criteria.

Your retirement needs to first accommodate your day-to-day income needs. How much money do you need to maintain your lifestyle? When do you need it?

Managing your risk by having a balance of Hope So Money vs. Know So Money is a good start that will put you ahead of the curve. But how much Know So Money is enough to secure your income needs during retirement, and how much Hope So Money is enough to allow you to continue to benefit from an improving market?

In short, how do you begin to know how much risk you should be exposed to?

While there is no single approach to investment risk determination advice that is universally applicable to everyone, there are some helpful guidelines. One of the most useful is called *The Rule of 100*.

The average investor needs to accumulate assets to create a retirement plan that provides income during retirement and also allows for legacy planning. To accomplish this, they need to balance the amount of risk to which they are exposed. Risk is required because, while Know So Money is safer, more reliable and more dependable, it doesn't grow very fast, if at all. Today's historically low interest rates barely break even with current inflation. Hope So Money, while less dependable, has more potential for growth. Hope So Money can eventually become Know So Money once you move it to an investment with lower risk. Everyone's risk diversification will be different depending on their goals, age and their existing assets.

So how do you decide how much risk your assets should be exposed to? Where do you begin? Luckily, there's a guideline you can use to start making decisions about risk management. It's called the Rule of 100.

APPLYING THE RULE OF 100

The Rule of 100 is a general rule that helps shape asset diversification* for the average investor. The rule states that the number 100

---

* *Asset Diversification disclosure – Diversification and asset allocation does not assure of or guarantee better performance and cannot eliminate the risk of investment loss. Before investing, you should carefully read the applicable volatility disclosure for each of the underlying funds, which can be found in the current prospectus.*

minus an investor's age equals the amount of assets they should have exposed to risk.

The Rule of 100: 100 - (your age) = the percentage of your assets that should be exposed to risk (Hope So Money)

For example, if you are a 30-year-old investor, the Rule of 100 would indicate that you should be focusing on investing primarily in the market and taking on a substantial amount of risk in your portfolio. The Rule of 100 suggests that 70 percent of your investments should be exposed to risk.

$$100 - (30 \text{ years of age}) = 70 \text{ percent}$$

Now, not every 30-year-old should have exactly 70 percent of their assets in mutual funds and stocks. The Rule of 100 is based on your chronological age, not your "financial age," which could vary based on your investment experience, your aversion or acceptance of risk and other factors. While this rule isn't an ironclad solution to anyone's finances, it's a pretty good place to start. Once you've taken the time to look at your assets with a professional to determine your risk exposure, you can use the Rule of 100 to make changes that put you in a more stable investment position—one that reflects your comfort level.

Perhaps when you were age 30 and starting your career, like in the example above, it made sense to have 70 percent of your

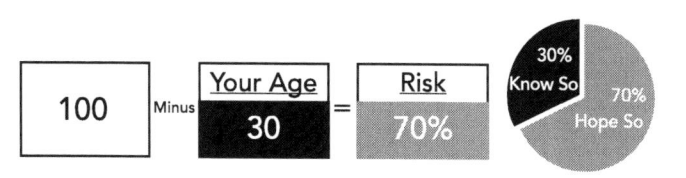

money in the market: you had time on your side. You had plenty of time to save more money, work more and recover from a downturn in the market. Retirement was ages away, and your earning power was increasing. And indeed, younger investors should take on more risk for exactly those reasons. The potential reward of long-term involvement in the market outweighs the risk of investing when you are young.

Risk tolerance generally reduces as you get older, however. If you are 40 years old and lose 30 percent of your portfolio in a market downturn this year, you have 20 or 30 years to recover it. If you are 68 years old, you have five to 10 years (or less) to make the same recovery. That new circumstance changes your whole retirement perspective. At age 68, it's likely that you simply aren't as interested in suffering through a tough stock market. There is less time to recover from downturns, and the stakes are higher. The money you have saved is money you will soon need to provide you with income, or is money that you already need to meet your income demands.

Much of the flexibility that comes with investing earlier in life is related to *compounding*. Compounded earnings can be incredibly powerful over time. The longer your money has time to compound, the greater your wealth will be. This is what most people talk about when they refer to putting their money to work. This is also why the Rule of 100 favors risk for the young. If you start investing when you are young, you can invest smaller amounts of money in a more aggressive fashion because you have the potential to make a profit in a rising market and you can harness the power of compounding earnings. When you are 40, 50 or 60 years old, that potential becomes less and less and you are forced to have more money at lower amounts of risk to realize the same returns. **It basically becomes more expensive to prudently invest the older you get.**

You risk not having a recovery period the older you get, so should have less of your assets at risk in volatile investments. You should shift with the Rule of 100 to protect your assets and ensure that they will provide you with the income you need in retirement. Let's look at another example that illustrates how the Rule of 100 becomes more critical as you age. An 80-year-old investor who is retired and is relying on retirement assets for income, for example, needs to depend on a solid amount of Know So Money. The Rule of 100 says an 80-year-old investor should have a maximum of 20 percent of his or her assets at risk. Depending on the investor's financial position, even less risk exposure may be required. You are the only person who can make this kind of determination, but the Rule of 100 can help. Everyone has their own level of comfort. Your Rule of 100 results will be based on your values and attitudes as well as your comfort with risk.

The Rule of 100 can apply to overarching financial management and to specific investment products that you own as well. Take the 401(k) for example. Many people have them, but not many people understand how their money is allocated within their 401(k). An employer may have someone who comes in once a year and explains the models and options that employees can choose from, but that's as much guidance as most 401(k) holders get. Many 401(k) options include target date funds that change their risk exposure over time, essentially following a form of the Rule of 100. Selecting one of these options can often be a good

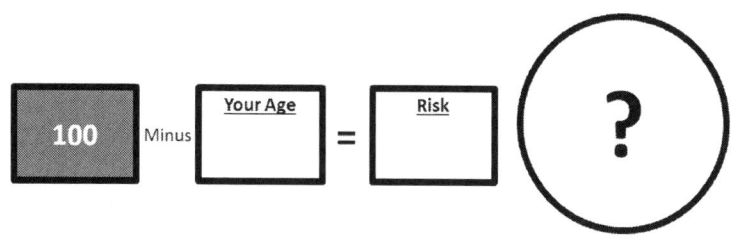

move for employees because they shift your risk as you age, securing more Know So Money when you need it. A financial professional can look at your assets with you and discuss alternatives to optimize your balance between Know So and Hope So Money.

CHAPTER 1 RECAP //
- Your retirement plan should begin not with your money, but with your ideas about what an ideal retirement looks like to you. What are some of the things you have always wanted to do but never had the time to do because you had to go to work?
- Knowing what to do with your retirement savings begins with understanding that the investment strategies used to GET you to retirement are different from the ones that you need to STAY secure in retirement.
- There is money you hope you'll have in the future, and there's money you know you'll have in the future. Make sure you know how much you need when you retire.
- Organizing your assets starts with making a list. You can then understand how each asset is balanced for risk.
- Your exposure to risk is ultimately determined by you.
- Use the Rule of 100 as a general guiding principle when determining how much risk your retirement investments should be exposed to (100 - [your age] = [percentage of your investments that can comfortably exposed to risk])

2
AN EXAMINATION OF RISK

We know from research that most people's greatest fear is running out of money before their life is done.

Having an overly optimistic view about the market's performance and its ability to generate sustainable income going forward is the biggest mistake we see people making as they move from their working years to retirement. Too many people enter into retirement high on the wave of their accumulation years, unprepared for the realities of their distribution years. They are counting on unrealistic returns as part of their income plan, and they take on far more risk than they realize. One bad loss and things can quickly come crashing down.

We know from research that most people's greatest fear is running out of money before their life is done. Taking the time now to examine your retirement savings from a risk standpoint will help make sure this doesn't happen to you. We talked earlier about the difference between *getting there* and *staying there* when it comes to retirement. This chapter is dedicated to a thorough examination of risk.

THE COLORS OF MONEY

Over the course of your lifetime, it is likely that you have acquired a variety of assets. Assets can range from money that you have in a savings account or a 401(k), to a pension or an IRA. You have earned money and have made financial decisions based on the best information you had at the time. When viewed as a whole, however, you might not have an overall strategy for the management of your assets.

As we have seen, it's more important than ever to know which of your assets are at risk. High market volatility and low treasury rates make for challenging financial topography. Even if you feel that you have plenty of money in your 401(k) or IRA, not knowing how much *risk* those investments are exposed to can cause you major financial suffering. Take the market crash of 2008 for example. In 2008, the average investor lost 30 percent of their 401(k). If more people had shifted their investments away from risk as they neared retirement age (i.e. the Rule of 100), they may have lost a lot less money going into retirement.

It can be helpful to assign colors to the different kinds of money and their level of risk to give you a visual schematic of where you currently stand.
- Green Money is Know So Money, which is safer and more dependable.
- Red Money is Hope So Money, which is exposed to risk and fluctuates with the market.

Green Money	Red Money
"Green Money" is safer.	"Red Money" is at risk.
This is money that offers a minimum guarantee but it may pose risks other than market risk.	This is money that can go up or down in value. It may pose risk if it is not properly managed to serve a specific purpose in a comprehensive plan.

A financial professional can help you better understand the color of the money in your investment portfolio.

The fact of the matter is that a lot of people don't know their level of exposure to risk. Visually organizing your assets is an important and powerful way to get a clear picture of what kind of money you have, where it is and how you can best use it in the future. This process is as simple as listing your assets and assigning them a color based on their status as Know So or Hope So Money. Work with your financial professional to create a comprehensive inventory of your assets to understand what you are working with before making any decisions. This may be the first time you have ever sat down and sorted out all of your assets, allowing you to see how much money you have at risk in the market. Comparing the color of your investments will give you an idea of how near or far you are from adhering to the Rule of 100.

FINDING THE RIGHT BALANCE

The next step is to know the right amount and ratio of Green and Red Money for you at your stage of retirement planning.

Investing heavily in Red Money and gambling all of your assets on the market is incredibly risky no matter where you fall within the Rule of 100. Money in the market can't be depended on to generate income, and a plan that leans too heavily on Red Money can easily fail, especially when investment decisions are influenced by emotional reactions to market downturns and recoveries. Not only is this an unwise plan, it can be incredibly stressful to an investor who is gambling everything on stocks and mutual funds.

But a plan that uses too much Green Money avoids all volatility and can also fail. Why? Investing all of your money in Certificates of Deposit (CDs), savings accounts, money markets and other low return accounts may provide interest and income, but that likely won't be enough to keep pace with inflation. If you focus exclusively on income from Green Money and avoid owning any stocks or mutual funds in your portfolio, you won't be able to leverage the potential for long-term growth your portfolio needs to stay healthy and productive.

This is where working with a financial professional becomes crucial to the longevity of your plan. While the Rule of 100 can help you determine how much of your money should be invested in the market to anticipate your future needs, it doesn't tell you what strategies to use and how to best optimize the strengths of your individual portfolio. **Many people make mistakes in this area of risk due to simple lack of education.** They don't realize how much risk they are exposed to, how much risk they need or what other options are available. Almost all retirees need the professional guidance of a qualified retirement planning advisor to help them strike the right balance. Many do it yourself (DIY) retirees either make the mistake of taking too much risk or not taking enough risk to stay ahead of inflation's effects. This planning is too crucial to leave to chance. This is one thing you definitely want to do right, from the beginning.

We often use a planning technique we call a *hybrid strategy* that can give you adequate growth without the risk of loss. This strategy can also go to work for you by combating other risks that aren't related to the stock market, such as the risk of inflation and the cost of long-term care. These are the risks associated with the perks of living longer. Being aware of these risks can help you put your game face on so you can better handle all the curve balls retirement might throw you.

THE GREAT MAGNIFYER: LONGEVITY RISK

As an employee with a 401(k) plan or the Federal Thrift Saving Plan (TSP), you have been in charge of growing and saving your own retirement fund. This has resulted in a focus on growth and accumulation. During retirement, however, it's not about the ability of an investment to generate a return; it's about income. How do you take that half a million dollars in your TSP and turn it into an income for the next 20 or more years?

Perhaps the trickiest thing about retiring today is how the issue of longevity magnifies exponentially any and all other risks.

Your chances of running out of income increase when you take on one or more of the following risks: market loss, inflation and the cost of long-term care. When magnified by living longer, these risks can quickly and dramatically drain away your assets. We want to be as comprehensive as possible when considering the threats to your future, which is why we take a look at all the risks under the magnifying glass of longevity so that we can better plan for the realities ahead.

Market Risk: Most people are familiar with the fluctuations of the stock market and how those big swings can contribute to loss of funds. During retirement, you have two things working against you: one, you no longer have the ability to replenish those funds with the automatic deductions taken from your paycheck; and two, because you need this money to provide an income, you can't wait until the market recovers before making withdrawals. When you look at this risk under the longevity magnifier, imagine what would happen to a $100,000 portfolio that sustained a 40 percent loss during the first year of a 20-year retirement.

Inflation Risk: This is one of the most under-discussed of all the risks, and the fact that we are living longer points directly to its relevance. Growing your savings so they can keep up with inflation isn't as easy as it once used to be. Low-risk vehicles such as bank CDs used to earn enough interest to at least break even with inflation. Now, relying on those types of vehicles to drive the long distance of today's retirement can lead to a phenomenon we in the industry refer to as, *going broke safely.*

Public Policy Risk: This is the risk to your plan that occurs when politicians change the game. One example that can affect your income during retirement has to do with Social Security. As of the writing of this book, section 831 of the House's new budget bill passed changes to the way Social Security provides spousal and retirement benefits.* This isn't the first time we have seen changes to the Social Security program. When setting up your income plan, you want to control as many things as you can in order to ensure you will have the income you need, when you need it.

Long-term Care Risk: Most natural transitions in life happen gradually over time, and aging is a prime example. As we get older, our bodies get tired and start to wear out. Long-term care doesn't just refer to the services we need at the end of life due to chronic illness. It can also refer to basic custodial services such as housekeeping and grocery shopping. **The U.S. Department of Health and Human Services reports that nearly 70 percent of senior citizens turning 65 years old will need some form of long-term care during their lives.**** What is your strategy for funding this?

---

* *http://www.pbs.org/newshour/making-sense/houses-proposed-budget-bill-will-devastating-effects-millions-social-security-benefits/?utm_source=facebook&utm_medium=pbsofficial&utm_campaign=newshour*

** *http://longtermcare.gov/the-basics/*

LONG-TERM CARE STRATEGIES

If you ask the average retiree today what his or her plan for long-term care is, they might tell you, "My plan is a Smith & Wesson." While this is usually meant to be a joke, statistics point to the fact that for married couples, chances are pretty good one of you is going to have to bite the bullet and make some difficult decisions. While the subject of spousal planning will be covered in the next chapter, long-term care planning bears mentioning here because many people underestimate just how long they will live. About one out of every four 65-year-olds can expect to live past the age of 90, and one out of 10 will live past the age of 95.* These bonus years granted to us by the angel of longevity can be either a problem or an opportunity. So ask yourself, really, *"What is my plan?"*

Consider the following four options and have a conversation with your financial professional to decide what will work best for your situation.

Option #1: Self-funding: If you have the assets and don't mind writing out large checks, you can choose to self-fund the cost of long-term care. While the cost of care varies depending on the types of services needed, the median average in the state of Idaho for a semi-private room (double-occupancy) is $6,935 per person, per month.** Given that men need care for an average of 2.2 years and women need care longer (3.7 years), how long would you be able to continue footing the bill?***

Option #2: Medicaid: If you choose option #1 as your plan for long-term care, you might find that you end up depleting your assets. Medicaid is a joint federal and state program that can help pay for costs associated with medical and long-term care, but there are strict eligibility requirements based on income and

---

* http://ssa.gov/planners/lifeexpectancy.htm
** http://www.skillednursingfacilities.org/resources/nursing-home-costs/
*** http://longtermcare.gov/the-basics/how-much-care-will-you-need/

asset limits. *Medicaid spend down* is a term that refers to legally divesting yourself of your assets in order to qualify for Medicaid's funding of long-term care. If you are thinking of qualifying for Medicaid as part of your long-term care strategy, then you will want to speak to an elder care law attorney who specializes in Medicaid law.

Option #3: Traditional Long-term Care Insurance: Most people are familiar with the traditional long-term care insurance programs first offered by life insurance companies back in the 1980s. These programs have many pros and cons to be aware of, and they do get more difficult to qualify for as you age. Federal employees have access to group plans that can be easier to qualify for. Should you be one of the lucky 30 percent who never need care, however, all the money you pay into the plan is lost to the insurance company.

Option #4: The Combo-plan: In the fast-food industry, combo-plans are a good way to get a satisfying deal, and the insurance industry has picked up on that. Their combination, or hybrid, plans have become very popular. They offer a leveraged death benefit combined with long-term care benefits. Annuities are also offering long-term care benefit features available with the purchase of a rider. This can be an excellent option for any money you have languishing away in a low-earning CD. Plop down a sum of money into a single-premium life insurance plan or an annuity with a rider, and you can get a two-for-one deal, so to speak: earning higher returns while setting aside funds for long-term care. Best of all, should you never get sick and need the care, any money you don't use reverts back to your named beneficiaries.

WORKING WITH A QUALIFIED RETIREMENT PROFESSIONAL

As you leave your working years behind and enter into retirement, you are also leaving your accumulation years. Your investment

focus changes from the rate of return to the amount of income the investment can produce. Take a moment to think about your income goals:
- What is your lifestyle today?
- Would you like to maintain it into retirement?
- Are you meeting your needs?
- Are you happy with your lifestyle?
- What do you really *need* to live on when you retire?

Some people will have the luxury of maintaining or improving their lifestyle, while others may have to make decisions about what they need versus what they want during their retirement. **The better understanding you have of your current position and the risks associated with that position, the better your chances for success.** Organizing your assets, understanding the color of your money, and creating an income and accumulation plan for retirement can quickly become an overwhelming task. The fact of the matter is that financial professionals build their careers around understanding the different variables affecting retirement financing. Registered Investment Advisors specifically specialize in the creation of a holistic plan that takes into account all the working parts of your plan. If you have a three-legged retirement income stool made up of your pension, Social Security benefit, and a defined-contribution benefit, wouldn't you want to know if one of those legs is weak as a toothpick? Nobody wants to go into retirement sitting on a broken stool.

Working with a Registered Investment Advisor means working with a professional who is legally obligated to help you make financial decisions that are in your best interest and fall within your comfort zone. Working with a Trained Federal Benefits Consultant means working with a professional who has taken classes and understands the intricacies involved when coordinating federal benefits. Taking steps toward creating a retirement plan is nothing to take lightly. By understanding how you are positioned for risk, properly organizing your assets, and accumulating helpful financial strategies that help you meet your income and accumulation needs, you are more likely to build a plan strong enough to support you for the duration of your retirement. You might have a million dollars socked away in a savings account, but your neighbor, who has $300,000 in a diverse investment portfolio that is tailored to their needs, may end up enjoying a better retirement lifestyle. Why? They had more than a good work ethic and a penchant for saving. They had a planned approach to retirement asset allocation.

CHAPTER 2 RECAP //

- Assign colors to your investments to help you easily visualize the assets that make up your retirement savings. Green Money is made up of safer, more reliable *Know So* investments. Red Money represents assets that are exposed to risk and can also be thought of as *Hope So* investments.
- The issue of longevity serves as a magnifier for all other risks: market risk, inflation, policy risk and the risk of long-term care.
- Addressing long-term care now can give you more control over your retirement. You basically have four options when it comes to paying for long-term care: self-insure, Medicaid, traditional long-term care insurance, or the new Combo-plans offered by life insurance companies.
- Working with a Registered Investment Advisor will help you compose a clear and concise inventory of your assets, learn how much they are worth, what rules apply to them, and how they are structured for risk. An Investment Advisor is legally obligated to help you make financial decisions that are in your best interest and fall within your comfort zone.

3
REVIEWING YOUR INCOME NEEDS

Will we have enough money for retirement?

An important aspect of your financial plan is the evaluation of your income needs. Finding the most efficient and beneficial way to address them will impact your lifestyle, your asset accumulation and your legacy planning. When you have identified your income need, you will know how much of your savings is to be structured towards income and how much is to be set aside for accumulation.

Every financial strategy for retirement needs first to accommodate the day-to-day need for income. The moment your working income ceases and you start living off the money you've set aside for retirement is referred to as the **retirement cliff**. When you begin drawing income from your retirement assets, you have entered the distribution phase of your financial plan. ***The distribution phase of your retirement plan*** is when you reach the point of relying on your assets for income. This is where your Green Money comes into play: the safer, more reliable assets that you have accumulated that are designed to provide you with a steady income.

On day one of your retirement, you will need a steady and reliable supply of income from your Green Money. The thing to keep in mind, however, is that you don't know how long you will need this money for. Additionally, your spouse may have need of the income longer than you do. A good plan takes all of this into consideration

HOW MUCH DO YOU NEED?

It can be a little scary to think about the day you step into retirement and your paycheck stops coming. Will your savings be enough to provide you with a replacement check? Satisfying that need for daily income requires a review of ***how much you need*** and ***when you will need it,*** but that's not all. We also need to look at the life factors that can affect how much you will need and when, and who you will need that money for.

How much money do you need to fund your lifestyle? You will want to consider the things you would like to be doing, as well as any risks you want to prepare for now, such as funding long-term care.

While this amount will be different for everyone, the general rule of thumb is that a retiree will require 90 to 100 percent of their *net* income. Most people enter into retirement with good savings habits. During their working years, a portion of every paycheck was automatically set aside or deducted to fund a retirement plan, a 401(k) or a TSP. There was also a portion of your paycheck deducted for Social Security and for Medicare. Once you retire, you no longer need to fund those accounts, because you are no longer *getting there*. Instead, you have arrived.

How much of your salary did you actually take home? What are you used to living on? What expenses do you expect to change? For example, do you have any existing debt that you plan to have paid off?

What if you haven't saved enough? Many people underestimate how much money is required to generate the income they need. During the last five or so years before retirement, there is a lot you can do to catch up if you meet with a financial professional and learn how to maximize your opportunities. Many defined-contribution plans such as the Thrift Saving Plan and the 401(k) have catch-up provisions, and the IRS also has new rules to help people put away more money. As you approach retirement, many people find they are at their peak earning years and the kids are out of the house. With a little bit of planning, you can design your income plan ahead of time to ensure a smooth and stress-free transition between the *getting there* and *staying there* years.

When Do You Need Your Money? Money that you need to depend on for income is Green Money. Green Money becomes much more important as you age. While you want to reduce the amount of Red Money you have and to transition it to Green Money, you don't necessarily need all of it to generate income for you right away. Taking a closer look at your income needs, you will see that you don't actually need all of your money to generate income right away.

YOUR HYBRID RETIREMENT: *GO-GO, SLOW-GO AND NO-GO*

Most people find they need more than just Green Money to supply their income needs due to the increased length of retirement. We talked earlier about investments for long-term growth. In order to meet those long-term growth needs, you might need to rely on what we call a hybrid retirement. A hybrid retirement uses a little bit of this and a little bit of that until we get an income plan that's just right for you.

Generally speaking, there are two types of Green Money: money used for income now and money used for accumulation to meet your income needs in five, 10 or 20 years.

Money needed for income is Need Now Money. It is money you need to meet your basic needs, to pay your bills, your mortgage if you have one and the costs associated with maintaining your lifestyle.

Money used for accumulation is Need Later Money. It's money that you don't need now for income, but will need to rely on down the road. This might still be Green Money because you will rely on it later for income and will need to count on it being there, or you might rely on the managed money strategies talked about in Chapter 8, *Why You Should Consider Managed Money.*

Need Later Money represents income your assets will need to generate for future use. When planning your retirement, it is vital to decide how much of your assets to structure for income now and how much to set aside to accumulate to create Need Later Money. How much growth you need is determined in large part by your income needs.

To help you determine how much money to set aside for future needs, industry speaker and expert Tom Hegna, author of, "Don't Worry, Retire Happy!" talks about the three phases in retirement. These three-phases might sound oversimplified, but they make sense when used as a guideline to consider your Need Now and Need Later income needs.

The Go-Go Phase represents the first 10 or so years of retirement when you have things you want to do such as see the world or start a new business. It's also the first time in your life where every day is Saturday, you might feel like celebrating during what could potentially be the most fun and rewarding stage of your life. You're feeling young and strong and you want to get on with all the things you've always wanted to do but never could, due to work commitments. Now you've got both the time and the energy; with proper planning, you can also ensure ample funds.

The Slow-Go Phase usually happens sometime around your mid-70s after you have gotten a lot done and are feeling like you might want to slow things down. Maybe it's that you appreciate the simple things in life more deeply, such as time with old friends or quiet evenings with your spouse. Maybe it's that you have a few aches and pains settling in. Regardless of the why, the Slow-Go phase can be a peaceful time of enriched experiences and relationships. You no longer need to fund expensive trips or excursions, the kids have finished college and your needs are simplified. This is the time in your life when your expenses may see a slight decrease.

The No-Go Phase might sneak up on you slowly or it might happen all at once due to an illness. As you enjoy the increased longevity that medical science has gifted to us, you might also find yourself more aware of your limitations. This is the stage where health issues might start to crop up and where it might be necessary to fund some sort of long-term care. According to the U.S. Department of Health and Human Services, 69 percent of people over the age of 90 have a disability.* Most people prefer to stay in their home for as long as possible. A solid income plan that addresses the realities of the No-Go years can give you more choices when it comes to your health care.

HAVE YOU PLANNED FOR YOUR SPOUSE?

With traditional defined-benefit pension plans, the income goes away when the person passes away, which means you will lose more than just your spouse: you lose your income. If you are receiving one or more pensions as part of your income during

---

* *http://longtermcare.gov/the-basics/who-needs-care/*

retirement, then you will want to take a good look at the numbers when designing your spousal continuation plan.

Spousal continuation is the part of your income plan that takes a look at how much your income will drop when your spouse passes away. Social Security is another type of defined-benefit plan that ends once a person is deceased. Spousal benefit provisions under Social Security allow you the option of choosing the larger of the two benefit amounts should your spouse pass away. When this happens, you will only be getting one check, instead of the two you were previously getting. How would this affect your ability to pay the bills?

Most federal employees also receive some type of defined-benefit pension. A lot of people aren't even aware that their pension benefit comes with survivor benefits. These survivor benefits give you the option of receiving a lower income per month to supply an ongoing income for your spouse after your death. Most pensions offer these choices of receiving either the full pension amount, or a partial amount in exchange for a spousal pension. This could give your spouse anywhere from 100 percent to 25 percent of your normal pension income amount. For federal employees especially, this can be a tricky decision. Continuing Health insurance might also be tied into the picture; in other cases, you may be able to get much more for your money by using life insurance to cover the income gap.

Whether or not you have a pension decision to make regarding spousal benefits, you will want to consider the following list when thinking through your joint-income plan:
- The age difference between you and your spouse
- The longevity difference between you and your spouse (women tend to outlive men by an average of five years)*
- Age of dependent children

---

* *http://www.ssa.gov/policy/docs/ssb/v65n3/v65n3p31.html*

- The amount of debt owed by your estate
- The longevity that runs in the family, both yours and your spouse
- The current health of both you and your spouse

Using life insurance as an alternative to pension benefits can provide more flexibility for the same or fewer number of dollars. These policies give you the ability to provide your spouse with a larger chunk of tax-free money, plus you have the ability to change the beneficiary designations and provide a greater legacy to your loved one. Chapter 4 covers the strategies federal employees need to be aware of when considering pension benefits. Chapter 14 talks about the multiple benefits of using life insurance as a legacy tool.

CHAPTER 3 RECAP //
- The foundation of a retirement strategy depends on knowing how much money you need, when you need it and who you need it for.
- Using a hybrid approach to your income needs allows you to plan for Need Now and Need Later Money. Having a long-term growth plan in place is essential due to the surprising issue of longevity.
- The Go-Go phase represents the first years of retirement when you are more active and most likely to spend more money. The Slow-Go years are when you start slowing down and spending less. The No-Go years are when health issues might start to crop up.
- Spousal continuation is one area often overlooked by retirees. When one spouse dies, the loss of pensions and monetary benefits such as Social Security means a reduction in monthly income. Your income plan should take into consideration guaranteed sources of income that will still be available after your spouse passes away.

4
STRATEGIES FOR FEDERAL EMPLOYEES

When is the best time to retire?

For Federal employees who will be retiring under one of the two retirement systems, either as a CSRS or FERS, you have a lot of decisions to make about your TSP, your pension election, survivor benefits, health insurance and life insurance plans. Learning how to work within the rules of the system to make the best choices possible is what we in the business refer to as a strategy. There is more to retiring than simply putting your initials in the box and sending in your paperwork. Every decision you make affects other areas of your retirement such as your taxes, your ability to access your money and your exposure to risk; pension election decisions also affect your health insurance eligibility and the ability of your spouse to pay the bills once you are no longer around; even your sick leave, credible service and the day that you retire can make a difference between more or less income during retirement. **These decisions matter, and for the most part, you only get to make them once.** That's why it's worth taking the time now to acquaint yourself with strategies that can help you get the very most out of the retirement you have worked so hard to earn.

The following information is by no means an exhaustive explanation of Federal benefits, but rather is designed to give you an idea of what might be possible when working under the guidance of a knowledgeable professional trained in the area of Federal retirement benefits.

SUBMITTING A HEALTHY PACKAGE

Before you can begin receiving your Federal benefits, there are several forms that have to be filled out, some by you and others by your employer. On these forms, you will be making important decisions about:

- Your spousal survivor benefits;
- Federal Employees Health Benefits (FEHB);
- Federal Employees Group Life Insurance (FEGLI).

You will also be providing information about:

- Your military service;
- Individual Retirement Record (IRR) for all periods of covered service.

The Office of Personnel Management (OPM) defines a "healthy" package as one that is complete and accurate, and a package that has been checked for missing, inaccurate and inconsistent information. All forms must be completed originals, signed and dated by the applicant in ink. Some parts of the package—such as spousal consent forms—require that the election be notarized by a notary public and that the spouse sign and date the form. One of the most common errors found in retirement packages is failure to document the five years of FEHB coverage. As a financial professional trained to provide federal benefit consultations, we would be happy to help review your application to make sure it's a healthy one.

ALERT: Even if you do submit a perfectly healthy application, you won't receive the full amount of your pension annuity starting day one. It takes anywhere from four to nine months for your Human Resources agency and the OPM office to coordinate their efforts, calculate and file your benefit paperwork. While they are getting their act together, you will receive what's known as an "interim annuity" payment. *This payment is estimated to be approximately 75 percent of what your actual annuity payments will be, and this is what you will normally receive for the first several months of your retirement.*

TIP: One strategy that can be very helpful when planning for this income gap is to properly calculate and plan for a lump-sum payout of your annual leave. We will cover the information behind this strategy under the heading, *When Is The Best Time To Retire?*

PENSION MAXIMIZATION: HOW MUCH WILL I GET?

Generally speaking, CSRS employees receive a substantial pension annuity and access to TSP and VCP benefits that don't have matching contributions, but only limited or no access to Social Security benefits. FERS employees receive a much smaller pension with matching contributions to their TSP and an amount they will receive from Social Security. Both plans contribute to Medicare and are eligible for FEHB and FEGLI benefits.

Your pension annuity, as defined earlier, simply refers to your annual payment.

There are only two components to the retirement pension annuity formula:

- Your "high-3" average salary years;
- Your service time.

How to calculate your pension benefits: For CSRS and FERS employees, annuity benefits are calculated using the highest average basic pay you earned during any three consecutive years of service. This is known as your "high-3" average pay. The formula multiplies a percentage of your salary to get a grand total for your annuity, which is then divided by 12 to calculate what your monthly payment will be. Your service time as it relates to your annuity pension pay is calculated differently depending on which program you are in.

For CSRS Employees: Generally speaking, the longer you have served, the earlier you can retire and receive an immediate pension, meaning payments will start 30 days after you stop working (but remember, this interim payment will be less than your actual payment.)

In addition to the following requirements, you must have served in a position subject to CSRS coverage for one of the last two years before your retirement in order to be eligible for an immediate pension. Your answer to the question, *"when can I retire,"* can be answered by looking at the following years of service thresholds:

- If you have served for 30 years, you can retire as early as age 55.
- If you have served 20 years, you can retire as early as 60.
- If you have served for only five years, the earliest you can retire is 62.

These are the guidelines if you want to receive your full pension benefits.

CSRS employees can choose to retire early, but there will be a 2 percent reduction to your pension benefit for each year

that you are under the age of 55. There are exceptions to this. For example, air traffic controllers can retire at any age once they have put in 25 years of service as an air traffic controller. Law enforcement and firefighter personnel, nuclear materials courier, Supreme Court Police and Capitol Police also have special provisions for early retirement.*

For FERS Employees: The rules for calculating and qualifying for a pension are different for FERS. Remember that for FERS employees, the pension is only one part of the three legs of the retirement stool. FERS employees will also have their Social Security benefit and the savings in their TSP or other qualified plan.

When it comes to receiving pension benefits, FERS employees need to have completed a minimum number of years of service as well as the minimum retirement age requirement. With FERS, however, your Minimum Retirement Age (known as your MRA) is based on the year of your birth. The following chart can be helpful when determining your MRA:

If your year of birth is:	Then your MRA is:
1948	55 and 2 months
1949	55 and 4 months
1950	55 and 6 months
1951	55 and 8 months
1952	55 and 10 months
1953-1964	56
1965	56 and 2 months
1966	56 and 4 months
1967	57 and 6 months
1968	58 and 8 months
1969	59 and 10 months
1970 and on	57

---

* *https://www.opm.gov/retirement-services/csrs-information/eligibility/*

You are eligible for your full pension benefits when the following happens:
- You have reached your MRA and served for 30 years.
- You have reached age 60 and served for 20 years.
- You have reached age 62 and have served for a minimum of five years.

You are eligible for early retirement when the following happens:
- You have reached your MRA and served for 10 years.

This early retirement is sometimes called the MRS +10 retirement, and you do want to be aware of the age reduction penalty: **There will be a 5 percent reduction for each year that you are under the age of age 62.*** This reduction isn't a one-time occurrence. The reduced amount is locked-in for the life of the pension. Depending on your other retirement assets, this may or may not be an issue for you. Your pension will NOT be reduced if you have completed at least 30 years of service, or if you completed at least 20 years of service by the time you reach age 60. Also note that even if you retire with a reduced pension amount, you are able to keep your Federal Employee Health Benefits (FEHB) assuming you have been enrolled in the program for at least 5 years immediately preceding retirement.

TIP: For FERS employees, your Social Security benefit is a big part of the three-legged stool, but be aware that the earliest age you can start receiving Social Security benefits is the age of 62. **FERS employees who retire before age 62 get a supplement that no one else receives called a FERS Special Supplement.** This supplement paid from age 57 to 62 is designed to help make

---

* *https://www.opm.gov/retirement-services/fers-information/types-of-retirement/#url=Early-Retirement*

up for the income gap you'll feel while waiting to have access to your Social Security benefit. Once you turn age 62, the Special Supplement stops.

ALERT: If you plan to work during retirement, be aware that Social Security puts a cap on your earnings after which you are assessed a penalty. If you are under the Full Retirement Age (FRA) for the entire year, you will be penalized $1 from your benefit payments for every $2 you earn above the annual limit. The annual limit for 2016 is $15,720. The year you reach FRA, the annual exempt amount for 2016 is $41,880. This higher exempt amount applies only to earnings made during the months prior to the month of FRA attainment.* The year after the FRA and beyond you can earn as much as you want with no penalty.

STRATEGIES TO INCREASE YOUR RETIREMENT PENSION

Just as any penalties to your annual pension amount are locked-in, so, too, are any increases to your pension. Given that the average 65-year-old is likely to live another 20 years, retiring at age 55 can mean 30 years of pension payments. Even just a small $50 increase in your monthly payment will pay you an additional $18,000 in lifetime income. Other strategies such as deferring your pension payment or diversifying your taxes can save you hundreds of thousands. This is where pension maximization strategies can really go to work in your favor.

Sick Leave
One area that federal employees will want to pay special attention to is getting credit for their unused sick leave. Federal employee "Sick Leave" benefits are said to be much more generous than

---

* https://www.ssa.gov/oact/cola/rtea.html

those of the private sector. Just to refresh your memory, here is a list of the sick leave benefits federal employees are entitled to:

- Full-time employees receive four hours of sick leave (the equivalent of a half day) for each pay period.
- Part-time employees get one hour of sick leave for each 20 hours worked in a pay status.
- There is NO LIMIT to the amount of sick leave that can be accumulated.
- Sick leave can be used for your own needs or to care for the needs of a family member.
- At retirement, any unused sick leave is added up, and this is where things can get interesting. Hours add up to days, which add up to weeks, and weeks add up to months and months add up to years.

When it comes time to calculate your years of service, your sick leave time is added to those years for the purpose of computing your retirement pay or annuity. That's why adding time to your service years by building up sick leave can have such a positive effect on your retirement pay. The more service years you have, the more money you will receive each month in retirement.

As part of your pension maximization strategy, you want to look at any unused sick leave to calculate how best to maximize those days. Should you spend them or save them? Do you have enough stored up to really make a difference? Pay special attention to how crediting your unused sick leave can beneficially affect your overall service time.

ALERT: Only whole months are used in the computation for sick leave. For example, if you have 30 years of service combined with one year, two months and 28 days of sick leave, the OPM would use 31 years and 2 months of service time in calculating your retirement annuity. The 28 days would not be included!

TIP: Take caution when computing your sick days and be sure to leave a small buffer in case of error. For example, using our situation above where an employee has 28 days of sick leave on the table, imagine what would happen if he or she decided to "burn up" those extra days, taking lots of time off just before retirement, only to find out later that the calculation was off by one or two days. Eeek! That error would then eat into the service time calculation of 31 years and 2 months and a lower monthly annuity payment would result.

Non-deducted Credible Civilian Service
Making sure you get credit for any unused sick leave is one strategy that can positively increase your monthly payment. Another way to impact that part of the formula is to make sure that you are getting *full credit for all of your service time*. Here are some of the categories of service you may need to consider:
- Part-time work
- Temporary work
- Seasonal employment
- Military service (even if you're receiving military retirement pay under special provisions)
- Refunded time (employee left federal service and withdrew retirement contributions)
- Workers compensation time and leave without pay.

If you have worked for any agency or performed service at any time in any of these capacities you should contact a qualified professional to help you work with your HR department to make sure you get credit for *all* your federal service. Consider the following story of how getting full credit for service time can make a difference to an aspiring retiree:

» The year he turned age 18, George went to work for the Bureau of Land Management as a fire fighter during the summer season. He found the work physically challenging and enjoyed working outside, so he returned for three more years every summer until he finished college and got his first job. Each summer he worked for 90 days, but because he was considered a seasonal employee, no money was withheld from his pay to go towards his Basic Benefit Plan. When George turned age 27, however, he was hired full-time by the U.S. Forestry Service.

George is now 55-years old and thinking about retirement. He plans to retire at age 57, at which time he will have served 30 years as a federal employee. His paycheck will be based on how many years he worked, and when he sits down to do the math himself, he comes up with a monthly pension amount of $2,110. But he also has those four years of summer service. How can he get those years of service worked into the equation? George also has a nice sum in his TSP plan and he knows he needs to do something with that money during retirement, so he comes in to talk with a financial professional who is trained in federal employee benefits.

In addition to structuring his TSP for income, liquidity and growth, the financial professional takes a look at how he can get George credit for his years of civilian service. He explains that the federal government had no idea that he was going to be joining the federal family back when he was going to college, but now he has the option of going back in time. He shows George how to work with payroll to figure out how much money he was making at the time, and then how to put that amount into the system to be used as part of his annuity payment.

Working with his financial professional to credit his civilian service and sick leave time, George finds that his pension *annuity will increase by $132 a month. Over the course of his estimated retired lifetime, that amounts to another $47,520 that George never would have gotten had he tried to figure this out on his own.*

Remember, when it comes to pension maximization, there are only two components to the retirement formula: your high-three average salary years and service time. Being proactive by taking the time to properly calculate your service time and adding back in any unused sick leave and years of credible civilian service can have a positive effect on your lifetime retirement pay.

TIP: Both CSRS and FERS have a specific form called "Certified Summary of Creditable Service". You should use this form at least a year prior to retirement to confirm that OPM has record of all your service time.

ALERT: Buying back or making a deposit for periods of "non-deducted creditable service" should be done as soon as possible because the amount you have to pay to receive credit is growing each year as interest is added to the total of the outstanding amount.

THE TSP: WHAT TO DO WITH YOUR RETIREMENT SAVINGS

The Thrift Savings Plan or TSP is one area of retirement planning that you have the most control over, and as such, it is also the area where people make the most mistakes.

If you are in the FERS retirement system, you'll be especially interested in finding the answer to the question of what to do with the money in your TSP. All of the other federal benefits including Social Security are *formula* driven. Meaning, you get to choose when you start them, but the payouts are based on predesigned formulas that you have no control over. With formula driven benefits, you only get to choose the timing of when you turn them on.

With the TSP, you have control of its three key components:
- You get to choose how much to contribute.
- You decide on what funds to invest in.
- You control how and when to distribute the funds.

Having this control is great if you make good choices and difficult at best if you don't know what you are doing. This is one area in particular where you definitely want to seek advice from a qualified financial professional to make sure your choices are done right. Everyone's situation and needs are different, so it doesn't make sense to get a "one size fits all" solution.

Unfortunately, there's a lot of advice out there that, though well intentioned, does nothing to address the individual. Many advisors claim to have experience in this area when they don't; similar canned advice can come from a radio show, co-worker, financial magazine or a newsletter. (For a more in-depth discussion on where you can go for the best advice, check out the section at the end of this chapter called, *Financial Self-Defense*.)

Before we get deep into the details of how to manage your TSP, it's important to remind ourselves what the objective of the TSP is in the first place. **The TSP, along with Social Security benefits and your Federal Pension, is one of the three legs of the three-legged stool of** *retirement income.* For many years the financial industry has focused a lot of retirement planning energy on accumulating the biggest nest egg possible in retirement accounts like the TSP. Because of this emphasis, many people have no idea how much is enough for them to save. "*How much is enough?*" seems subjective because it is. The descriptor "enough" will be different for everybody mainly because *the size* of the account is only one part of the equation.

It's easy to forget that the main point of accumulating the account is to create retirement income. The better question to ask is, "*How much income will I need from my TSP?*" Once you have established the income need, you can then figure out with greater accuracy how much you need in your portfolio in order to generate that target amount.

Your First TSP Decisions: How much should you contribute?
Of the three key decisions you have control over, **contributions** are perhaps the most important. No contributions = no retirement savings = no stable income. How can you sit comfortably through a 20 to 30-year retirement on a two legged stool? The biggest reason we hear for not contribution to the TSP is, *I can't afford it.* Before you decide not to contribute to the TSP or profit sharing plan offered by your employer, consider the following story:

> » *Stewart came in to see a financial professional because he was worried about having enough income during retirement. As the professional laid out all of his numbers, he noticed that Stewart had never contributed to his companies' profit sharing plan. The profits of this company were big, and the company had grown and been acquired by bigger and bigger companies. Each new company increased the value of what would have been in this plan.*
>
> *Since he had all the numbers right there, the professional ran a quick calculation and figured out that if Stewart had just contributed 5 percent of his income during his working career, that profit sharing plan would have been worth close to $1,500,000 when Stewart retired. Not too bad for a general laborer! When the financial professional asked him why he had never contributed to the plan, Steward replied, "We had a big family, and I never felt like I could afford it".*

> *The question is, how will Stewart afford retirement without that $1.5 million?*

Other reasons people give for not contributing to their TSP include:
"I don't know how to manage it."
"I don't understand it."
"I don't think I will need it."

The first point to make here is that in order to plan for stable retirement income, you need to contribute to your TSP or company profit sharing plan. Please begin as early as you can and contribute at least 5 percent to your plan. As soon as you do, the government matches the 5 percent (if you are in the FERS system) which gives you the equivalent of a 100 percent return on your money. Even though employees who are in the CSRS system don't get the match on their contributions, it is still a good idea to put away money in the TSP or the VCP (covered later in this chapter). This is money that you will not see in your paycheck so you won't miss it. Most employees who set this up right away never even miss the money, and many of them could contribute more than 5 percent without creating a financial hardship.

As your income increases and your obligations decrease along with the elimination of debt and your children's financial demands, you should consider putting in more. The important thing is to look at the income you will need and save with that goal in mind.

TIP: One helpful strategy that savvy Federal employees have shared with us over the years is to put your pay increases right into your TSP. Because you are used to living on what you have been bringing home, this approach helps to build your retirement savings in a pain-free way.

Your Second TSP Decisions: Which funds should you invest in?

The TSP offers a way to gain access to the market and opportunities for growth. The question of which funds to invest in is a hot topic. The best way to invest in your TSP will depend on several factors:

- How much of a risk taker are you?
- What is your risk tolerance?
- How close are you to retirement?
- How old are you?
- How experienced are you in investing?

When it comes to choosing investments, many federal employees behave like most other investors: they invest based on the emotions. **Investing this way guarantees you will almost always be wrong.** You buy the C Fund because it did great last year, but this year, the S Fund turns out to do better. The problem with investing this way is you are going forward into the future based on what just happened. This can be compared to driving a car by looking only in the rearview mirror. In other words, it's a good strategy for inviting an accident.

Because of the many investment mistakes and myths that are out there, we have become fans of the Life Cycle or L funds, particularly for those who are near or approaching retirement age. The L Fund is made up of all five of the TSP investments funds: C, F, G, I, and S. It utilizes something called target-date investing: the closer you get to a specified date, the more conservative the asset mix. You might think of this as a fund that manages your risk similar to The Rule of 100. This can help you avoid the rearview mirror mistakes that hurt so many TSP investors during the last decade.

TIP: Proper diversification in your TSP is more important than hitting the jackpot. You want to avoid having your TSP fund crushed right before you retire, when you need to have that money available for income.

Your Third TSP Decisions: How and when should you distribute the finds?

The TSP can be a wonderful savings program for accumulating a good retirement account, but once you *get* to retirement, you want to *stay there (Secure)*. When considering the distribution of your TSP funds, it becomes not only prudent, but necessary, to consider what phase of retirement you are in. This is perhaps the most difficult step for federal retirees who want to know what to do with their money at retirement. Generally speaking, you have three options:

1. **TSP Withdrawal Options:** Your TSP plan will offer you different options at retirement. You can choose to take a one-time withdrawal, a monthly withdrawal, or a life annuity.
    a. *The one-time withdrawal* is a lump-sum payment option where the federal government cuts you a nice big check. While this might be tempting, keep in mind that you owe taxes on every single penny of this money. Taking the lump-sum option usually results in a hefty tax bill that has to be paid all at once instead of being spread out over the course of your retirement years.
    b. *A monthly withdrawal* usually means the same thing as taking your retirement income using Red Money investments. Monthly payments are not structured within an annuity, and while they may offer higher monthly payments, they also come with the risk that corresponds to the funds your TSP is invested in and may run out before your death.

    c. *A life annuity* would be the equivalent of a Green Money retirement income. Though it is subject to the annuity rules and distribution limitations of the annuity contract.
    d. *A Combination of the above payouts is also available.*

2. **In-Service Age-based Withdrawal:** If you are still working and are over the age of 59 ½, you have the option to move the entire balance out of your TSP, one time, without penalty. For example, you can establish an IRA with the funds in your TSP and can make a one-time transfer of the TSP balance. Any funds accumulated after this transfer will have to stay in your TSP until you retire or separate from service. Remember that making this move does not close your TSP. If rolled to a qualified plan like an IRA this move will have no tax consequence.

3. **Outside Lifetime Income Alternatives**: The TSP offers a lifetime income option. Many people have a need to create a lifetime income, at least with a portion of their TSP fund. There are a variety of lifetime income options available outside the TSP. Many find better payouts and superior survivor benefits from plans outside the TSP. It would be a mistake not to look at these options outside the TSP before making this vitally important lifetime income decision.

One important advantage the TSP offers over IRA type plans is access to your money at age 55. IRA's and 401(k) funds are not available without a penalty until age 59.5. If you are under the age of 55 and are in law-enforcement or a fire fighter or air traffic controller, there are special distribution eligibility rules.

When it's all said and done, the options you choose and the timing of your TSP distribution should reflect your retirement goals. The TSP is only one leg of the retirement stool, but it's an important leg. Without it, your retirement could very well be unstable. This is one area in particular where you will want to seek advice from a financial professional who understands the intricacies of the federal retirement system and your specific retirement plan. Remember this is the leg of your retirement income stool that you have the most control over and therefore the most important decisions to make. You will always be glad you did it right.

THE SECRET SAUCE TO THE CSRS SAVINGS PLAN

While FERS employees rely heavily on their contributions to their TSP plan, CSRS employees have the option of making contributions to the TSP and another plan known as the VCP. The Voluntary Contributions Program (VCP) is a special provision offered to CSRS employees that is in many ways superior to the TSP and often underutilized.

In short, the VCP plan allows CSRS employees to contribute more money to their retirement where it can grow tax-deferred and be withdrawn later tax-free. ***You might think of the VCP as an investment vehicle that can basically "wash" the tax liability right off your money!*** There is no other way that we are aware of for an average investor to do this. The following story illustrates how the VCP can multiply your savings:

> » *Sam started working for BLM back in the days before Internet, cell phones and texting. He signed up for the CSRS federal employee benefit plan and was also lucky enough to marry a woman who had a good income and a penchant for saving. Over the years, Sam and his wife, Virginia, paid off their house and all their debts and built up a substantial emergency fund of $100,000. As Sam was nearing*

retirement, his uncle passed away and they also inherited $200,000. Sam and Virginia now had $300,000 sitting in a bank account earning less than 1 percent interest. They are concerned about the risk of market volatility and investing in the stock market, but they are also concerned about having enough money during retirement.

Looking for a better opportunity for this money, Sam and Virginia go in to talk to a financial professional who has experience working with federal employees. The professional takes a good look at their entire financial picture. He explains that their particular situation has them incurring a potentially large tax burden during retirement. With an already substantial retirement income coming from tax-qualified funds, adding more taxable income to the pot would not be ideal.

He then explained how the VCP could work for them as a tax-diversification strategy. They saw that by contributing this $300,000 to the VCP and then rolling it out to a Roth IRA, they could grow this money tax-deferred. Later on during retirement, they could use this Roth IRA to generate an additional income for life and never have to pay taxes on that money. By using a wise strategy and a good financial vehicle, Sam and Virginia were able to substantially increase their return on investment and create a stream of tax-free lifetime income. Another happy ending.

Even if you don't have a large pot of cash sitting around, contributing to a VCP plan can be part of a strategic tax-diversification plan. **It offers benefits that the TSP does not have.** Remember: Any money that you contribute to your TSP is done pre-tax, so both the interest earned and the principle is taxed upon withdrawal.

VCP contributions are done after tax, like a Roth IRA, but with higher contribution limits. The VCP is also better than a Roth TSP because of the much higher contribution limit. The money can safely sit in this investment and grow tax-deferred, meaning the gains are compounded annually. The real secret to this strategy is the Roth IRA—an investment vehicle that allows you to withdraw both the principle and interest tax-free after a certain amount of time. By starting out in the VCP, you can enjoy greater contribution limits; by ending up in the Roth, you can enjoy tax-free growth and withdrawals. This strategy has two parts, and the timing of the Roth IRA roll over is important, so be sure to work with a qualified financial professional. In other words, don't try this strategy at home! This is one area in particular where having a financial professional trained in the area of federal employee benefits can help you to maximize your benefit potential.

TIP: Your VCP contributions may not exceed 10 percent of the total basic pay you received during all of your federal service. In most instances, your VCP account will not earn interest beyond the date of your separation from federal service, which is why you want to have guidance prior to retirement when rolling it out to a Roth IRA.

SURVIVOR ANNUITIES

Pensions offer lifetime annuities that pay-out an income for the rest of your life. What this means is that unless you elect otherwise, in the event of your death, your pension money will disappear when you do. Survivorship options allow you to receive a smaller monthly check in exchange for an extension of your pension annuity to your named survivor.

You might think of this pension reduction as a way to "buy" life insurance for your spouse. For married couples who are combining their retirement benefits, it may be more cost effective to keep the pension whole and purchase an outside life insurance policy that gives you greater beneficiary options. Consider the following story:

> » *Roy wants to make sure that his wife, Linda, has an income after his death. She doesn't have a pension of her own because she stayed home, raising their three kids for 25 years, and he knows the responsible thing to do is to take care of her. Roy signs up for the survivorship option that gives Linda the highest income amount of $660 after his death. This costs Roy $200 a month, and his pension payment goes down to $1,000 a month.*
>
> *Roy faithfully pays the $2,400 a year and for 10 years he and Linda are happily retired. Then, unexpectedly, his wife passes away first. He has now paid $24,000 into her spousal benefit, but Linda has gone to heaven and everything is free there. All the money he paid out is non-recoverable and he can't leave any of it to his kids. Because she died first, the money stays in the system and is lost.*

It is more common to see the husband pass away first, but in many of those cases, you see the surviving spouse passes away shortly after, and again all the money paid into the system is lost and nothing goes to the kids or grandkids. Alternatively, a life insurance plan might give you more value for your dollar since you can change the beneficiary if needed. Using life insurance assures that someone will receive the money. Your advisor can tell you if this approach makes sense for you. .

One area to pay particular attention to as you shop around for the best plan is health insurance. **Your spouse's eligibility for FEHB depends on a survivor benefit.** No survivor annuity = no federal health insurance benefit after the employees death. This is of particular importance if you have a younger spouse who has no other access to health insurance. The unexpected termination of health insurance due to the death of a spouse can leave a gap in your coverage, and finding replacement coverage can be inferior and more expensive. Depending on which program you are in, it might be possible to use a strategy that accomplishes your objectives by keeping the pension annuity going at the smallest cost possible in order to fund the health insurance, and then funding an outside life insurance policy on the side to plan for spousal continuation.

This is where sitting down with a professional who is trained in federal employee benefits can really do you a big favor. How much your beneficiary will receive and how much that benefit will cost you depends on which federal program you are in and which election you choose. The following is an overview of your options.

For CSRS Employees:
For those receiving pension benefits under the old CSRS program, you basically have three survivorship options. The cost for this benefit comes out of your monthly pension amount. The more you want to leave your named beneficiary, the more it will cost you and the lower your monthly pension check will be. Your three options are as follows:
- **You can choose to leave your survivor 55 percent of your annuity.** The cost for this benefit choice will reduce your annuity by just under 10 percent. In the event of your death, your spouse will continue to be eligible for FEHB.
- **You can choose to fill in a specified dollar amount in place of your unreduced pension amount.** On the form, it would look like this: 55 percent of $_____. The amount you list cannot be greater than your pension amount, but it can be as low as one dollar. This may be

a good option for couples who need to keep their FEHB benefits. The cost for this benefit choice will be just under 10 percent of the amount you write in the blank.
- **You can choose to end the annuity upon your death.** If you select this choice, you would receive the full amount of your pension and your annuity will end upon your death. Your spouse will no longer be eligible for FEHB. There is no cost for this option.

ALERT: All CSRS employees will want to be aware of two acronyms: **GPO** which stands for Government Pension Offset, and **WEP** which stands for the Windfall Elimination Provision. GPO and WEP will affect the spousal benefits paid out as part of Social Security. Because CSRS employees are not eligible for Social Security benefits, if you pass away and leave a pension annuity for your spouse, this survivor benefit may reduce the amount of Social Security benefits they are currently receiving. Your financial professional or your HR can calculate what impact WEP and GPO will have to your Social Security benefit.

For FERS Employees:
For FERS employees, you have three options, and the cost reduction to your pension amount is calculated using a similar formula. The three options for FERS employees are as follows:
- **You can choose to end the annuity upon your death.** If you select this choice, no survivor annuity would be paid to your spouse or beneficiary, and your spouse will no longer be eligible for FEHB. There is no cost for this option.
- **You can choose to leave your survivor 25 percent of your annuity.** The cost for this benefit choice is 5 percent of the pension amount. In the event of your death, your spouse will receive an annual income equal to 25 percent

of your pension amount, and he or she would continue to be eligible for FEHB.
- **You can choose to leave your survivor 55 percent of your annuity.** The cost for this benefit choice is 10 percent of the pension amount. In the event of your death, your spouse will receive an annual income equal to 50 percent of your pension amount, and he or she would continue to be eligible for FEHB.

ALERT: Unless your spouse is also a federal employee, their access to benefits such as health insurance is tied to your pension annuity.

FEHB AND FEGLI CONSIDERATIONS

The **Federal Employees Health Benefits** (FEHB) Program became effective in 1960 and is the largest employer-sponsored group health insurance program in the world, covering over 9 million federal employees, retirees, former employees, family members, and former spouses. As a retiree, once you turn age 65, you become eligible for Medicare. For many federal employees who enjoy the benefits of FEHB, paying extra for certain Medicare programs beyond parts A and B is not necessary. For married couples who choose *not* to continue their FEHB benefits as part of their spousal continuation plan, Medicare parts C and D may enter into the picture later. Be sure you understand the cost and coverage associated with your FEHB and Medicare benefits and seek wise counsel when considering how to handle the election of your benefits.

The **Federal Employee Group Life Insurance** (FEGLI) was established in 1954 and is the largest group life insurance program in the world, covering over 4 million federal employees and retirees, as well as many of their family members. For many federal employees raising families, FEGLI functions as a pretty good plan, but many people don't realize that this is term coverage. It gets more expensive to keep the older you get, and the premiums increase every five years. We've seen people paying as much as $800 a month for their FEGLI plan and in many cases, it isn't the insurance that you need as you enter into retirement. **There are many reasons why you need to carry life insurance throughout your life, but many people don't have the coverage they think they have.** There are strategies that a financial professional trained in federal benefits can apply when designing your comprehensive retirement plan, so be sure to ask for a full review of all your current life insurance policies, including the FEGLI.

WHAT ABOUT ANNUAL LEAVE?

All federal employees receive annual leave. The amount of annual leave you receive depends on your work status (see chart below*). Annual leave can be saved throughout the year and a maximum of 240 hours can be carried over into the next year, but it does not increase your years of service. Unlike sick leave, annual leave is not used to increase your retirement pay. **Instead, annual leave is paid out to you in a lump sum at retirement.**

EMPLOYEE TYPE	SERVICE LESS THAN 3 YEARS	SERVICE GREATER THAN 3 YEARS BUT LESS THAN 15 YEARS	SERVICE OF 15 OR MORE YEARS
FULL-TIME EMPLOYEE:	½ DAY (4 HOURS) FOR EACH PAY PERIOD	¾ DAY (6 HOURS) FOR EACH PAY PERIOD, EXCEPT 1 ¼ DAY (10 HOURS) IN THE LAST PAY PERIOD	1 DAY (8 HOURS) FOR EACH PAY PERIOD
PART-TIME EMPLOYEES:	1 HOUR FOR EACH 20 HOURS IN A PAY STATUS	1 HOUR FOR EACH 13 HOURS IN A PAY STATUS	1 HOUR FOR EACH 10 HOURS IN A PAY STATUS

Some special rules apply for Senior level, Scientific or Professional and Uncommon tour of duty personnel.

Earlier we discussed the process of applying for your retirement pension annuity. Remember: you will receive an "interim annuity" which is estimated to be approximately 75 percent of what your actual annuity payments will be for the first several months in retirement. For many retirees, the lump-sum payout of their annual leave will be important to help them get through these first several months while they receive only the interim annuity. There are strategies involved with *timing* your retirement that can help you to receive the maximum amount of this one-time payment.

For example: While only 240 hours can be carried over into the next year, if an employee who had 15 years or more of service planned their retirement for the 31st of December the following year, and they did not use any sick leave for that entire year, they would acquire eight hours each pay period, making a total of 208 hours for the year. Add that to the 240 hours carried over from the previous year, and they would be retiring with 448 hours of annual leave to be paid out to them. For many employees that could mean $10,000 to $15,000 of cash at retirement! This brings up the next million-dollar question: When is the best time to retire?

THE BEST TIME TO RETIRE

Many people puzzle over the chief question of when to retire in order to make the most out of their federal benefits. We always tell our clients: the best time to retire is when you are ready and when you want to! Of course, there are some things to consider that can help you to maximize your benefits, but generally speaking, these considerations should be viewed as a way to help you accomplish your goals, and not the goal itself.

CSRS employees can retire any of the first three days of the month or last day of the month, and their annuity accrual will begin the next day. If they retire on any other day, it will begin the 1st day of the following month. ***So if you retired in the middle***

of the month you could go as long as a month and a half before your annuity begins.

For FERS employees the annuity accrual always begins on the 1st of the month following retirement. Hence, **to get the maximum annuity you should retire the last day of the month.**

Some other considerations might be the lump-sum payout of your annual leave. If you retire at the end of the year, the payment for your annual leave will come the beginning of the following year. **Because you will be in retirement and most likely have a lower taxable income, it may be to your advantage to have the lump sum annual leave taxed in the year *after* your retirement so that you pay taxes at a lower rate.** Pay-periods may also be something to consider. You will not receive sick leave or annual leave for a pay period if you retire in the middle of that pay period.

In summation, for maximum credit you want to retire at the end of a pay period, when that pay period falls on the last day of December which also falls on the last day you want to work having used enough sick leave to "burn down" those extra days so you leave no "unused" sick leave days on the table. If you're a CSRS employee you want to make sure this all happens on one of the first three days of the month as well. If you are a FERS employee, you want to make sure it all happens on the last day of the month. It might as well be low tide and snowing in Hawaii too!

It's not just hard, but sometimes impossible to make all of this fall into place. After all, pay periods end when they end, and we cannot control whether or not it's the end of the month. That is exactly why we always say: "Retire when you're ready and when you want to!"

FINANCIAL SELF-DEFENSE

It used to be that Human Resource agencies had someone local you could go in and talk to when it came time to planning for retirement. When making these pension-election decisions, most people do need someone they can talk to face-to-face. These issues are complicated and tie into so many areas of personal life. Most federal employees can and do go to their HR department as their first point of contact, which is definitely good, but their advice can only take you so far. HR departments can only advise you on the one component of your federal benefits within your particular agency. **They cannot provide outside information about other resources or strategies that could greatly improve your financial position and affect the entire financial picture for your household.**

The Office of Personnel Management (OPM) website also provides answers to the most common questions, but many users find their website complicated and overwhelming. Finding the right answer to a particular question can be a bit like chasing a black cat down a dark alley, which is why you really want to sit down with someone in person. That being said, taking advice from a well-meaning financial professional who doesn't understand the complexities of how the federal retirement system works can also lead to a heap of trouble down the road if you aren't careful.

Getting good financial advice has become such an area of concern that the Certified Financial Planner Board (CFB), whose core mission is to serve the public, has published a financial self-defense guide. According to the CFP, as a current or aspiring retiree, you are in the age range most targeted for financial fraud. A 2009 survey by CERTIFIED FINANCIAL PLANNER™ professionals found that senior citizens lost a whopping $2.6 billion to bad advice and financial mismanagement according to the Elder Financial Planning Network.* By taking a defensive approach, you can be proactive rather than reactive when it comes to managing your finances.

---

* http://federalbenefitsadvice.com/wp-content/uploads/sites/96/cfpboard_financial_self-defense_guide.pdf

One self-defense move that can shield you from bad advice is to simply ask your financial professional to provide services with the "duty of care of a fiduciary." All Investment Advisor Representatives hold themselves to the fiduciary standards of liability. The U.S. Securities and Exchange Commission suggests that a trustworthy fiduciary advisor honors five major responsibilities when it comes to clients. Those responsibilities are:
- To put the clients' interests first;
- To act with utmost good faith;
- To provide full and fair disclosure of all material facts;
- Not to mislead clients; and
- To expose all conflicts of interest to clients.

Just as you can't board a plane without a boarding pass or proper identification, asking your financial professional for more information about their standards of liability and accreditation can help ensure that you are getting a plan that does the most to optimize your individual situation.

CHAPTER 4 RECAP //

- Participants in the FERS plan can think of their plan as having three legs like a stool. Those three legs include a smaller defined-benefit pension amount, access to Social Security benefits and access to matched funds within their TSP.
- You will be eligible for your benefits once you serve for a certain number of years and reach a certain age. Filing for your pension benefit early can result in a reduction penalty that is locked-in for the life of the pension. For FERS employees, your MRA is your Minimum Retirement Age based on the year of your birth.
- The TSP is very similar to a 401(k) plan for federal employees. Once you retire, you have three options when it comes to the withdrawal or distribution of your TSP fund.
- Participants in the CSRS plan and FERS have survivorship options. If you are married, be sure to select the option that considers the income and health insurance needs of your spouse in order to plan for spousal continuation.
- Any remaining sick leave time not used is added to your years of service for the purpose of computing your retirement pay or annuity. Annual leave is important when it comes to retirement but it cannot be used to increase your retirement pay.
- An Investment Advisor trained in federal employee benefits can help you determine when and how to file for your pension benefits as part of a coordinated and comprehensive retirement plan.

5
UNDERSTANDING SOCIAL SECURITY

One kind of Green Money that most Americans rely on for income when they retire is Social Security. If you're like most Americans, Social Security is or will be an important part of your retirement income and one that you should know how to properly manage. As a first step in creating your income plan, a financial professional will take a look at your Social Security benefit options. Social Security is the foundation of income planning for anyone who is about to retire and is a reliable source of Green Money in your overall income plan.

> » *Theresa had worked full-time nearly her entire adult life and was looking forward to enjoying retirement with her husband, kids and grandkids. When she turned 62, she decided*

to take advantage of her Social Security benefits as soon as they became available.

A couple of years later, she was organizing some of the paperwork in her home office. She came across an old Social Security statement, and remembered the feeling of filing and beginning a new phase in her life.

However, as she looked over the statement, she realized in retrospect that she might have been better off waiting to file for benefits. She had saved enough to wait for benefits, and if she had, her monthly benefit could have been quite a bit more.

When she was in the process of retiring, there were so many other decisions to make. It seemed very straightforward to file right away. She made a note to call the Social Security Administration to see if it was possible to change her monthly benefit to the larger amount.

Here are some facts that illustrate how Americans currently use Social Security:
- Nearly 90 percent of Americans age 65 and older receive Social Security benefits.*
- Social Security provides about 39 percent of the income of the elderly.*
- Claiming Social Security benefits at the wrong time can reduce your monthly benefit by up to 65 percent.**
- In 2013, 36 percent of men and 40 percent of women claimed Social Security benefits at age 62.***

---

* http://www.ssa.gov/pressoffice/basicfact.htm

** https://www.ssa.gov/planners/retire/retirechart.html

*** *Trends in Social Security Claiming*, Alicia H Munnell and Anqi Chen, Center for Retirement Research, May 2015. http://crr.bc.edu/wp-content/uploads/2015/05/IB_15-8.pdf

- In 2013, more than a third of workers claimed Social Security benefits as soon they became eligible.*
- In 2015, the average monthly Social Security benefit was $1,328. *The maximum benefit for 2015 was $2,663. The $1,335 monthly benefit reduction between the average and the maximum is applied for life.***

There are many aspects of Social Security that are well known and others that aren't. When it comes time for you to cash in on your Social Security benefit, you will have many options and choices. Social Security is a massive government program that manages retirement benefits for millions of people. Experts spend their entire careers understanding and analyzing it. Luckily, you don't have to understand all of the intricacies of Social Security to maximize its advantages. You simply need to know the best way to manage your Social Security benefit. You need to know exactly what to do to get the most from your Social Security benefit and when to do it. Taking the time to create a roadmap for your Social Security strategy will help ensure that you are able to exact your maximum benefit and efficiently coordinate it with the rest of your retirement plan.

There are many aspects of Social Security that you have no control over. You don't control how much you put into it, and you don't control what it's invested in or how the government manages it. However, you do control when and how you file for benefits. The real question about Social Security that you need to answer is, "When should I start taking Social Security?" While

---

* *Trends in Social Security Claiming, Alicia H Munnell and Anqi Chen, Center for Retirement Research, May 2015.* http://crr.bc.edu/wp-content/uploads/2015/05/IB_15-8.pdf

** https://www.ssa.gov/news/press/factsheets/colafacts2015.html

this is the all-important question, there are a couple of key pieces of information you need to track down first.

Before we get into a few calculations and strategies that can make all the difference, let's start by covering the basic information about Social Security which should give you an idea of where you stand. Just as the foundation of a house creates the stable platform for the rest of the framework to rest upon, your Social Security benefit is an important part of your overall retirement plan. The purpose of the information that follows is not to give an exhaustive explanation of how Social Security works, but to give you some tools and questions to start understanding how Social Security affects your retirement and how you can prepare for it.

Let's start with eligibility.

Eligibility. Understanding how and when you are eligible for Social Security benefits will help clarify what to expect when the time comes to claim them.

To receive retirement benefits from Social Security, you must earn eligibility. In almost all cases, Americans born after 1929 must earn 40 quarters of credit to be eligible to draw their Social Security retirement benefit. In 2015, a Social Security credit represents $1,220 earned in a calendar quarter. The number changes as it is indexed each year, but not drastically. In 2014, a credit represented $1,200. Four quarters of credit is the maximum number that can be earned each year. In 2015, an American would have had to earn at least $4,880 to accumulate four credits. In order to qualify for retirement benefits, you must have earned a minimum number of credits. Additionally, if you are at least 62 years old and have been married to a recipient of Social Security benefits for at least 12 months, you can choose to receive Spousal Benefits. Although 40 is the minimum number of credits required to begin drawing benefits, it is important to know that once you claim your Social Security benefit, there is no going back. Although there may be cost of living adjustments made, you are locked into that base benefit amount forever.

Primary Insurance Amount. You can think of your Primary Insurance Amount (PIA) like a ripening fruit. It represents the amount of your Social Security benefit at your Full Retirement Age (FRA). Your benefit becomes fully ripe at your FRA, and will neither reduce nor increase due to early or delayed retirement options. If you opt to take benefits before your FRA, however, your monthly benefit will be less than your PIA. You will essentially be picking an unripe fruit. On the one hand, waiting until after your FRA to access your benefits will increase your benefit beyond your PIA. On the other hand, you don't want the fruit to overripen, because every month you wait is one less check you get from the government.

Full Retirement Age. Your FRA is an important figure for anyone who is planning to rely on Social Security benefits in their retirement. Depending on when you were born, there is a specific age at which you will attain FRA. Your FRA is dictated by your year of birth and is the age at which you can begin receiving your full monthly benefit. Your FRA is important because it is half of the equation used to calculate your Social Security benefit. The other half of the equation is based on when you start taking benefits.

When Social Security was initially set up, the FRA was age 65, and it still is for people born before 1938. But as time has passed, the age for receiving full retirement benefits has increased. If you were born between 1938 and 1960, your full retirement age is somewhere on a sliding scale between 65 and 67. Anyone born in 1960 or later will now have to wait until age 67 for full benefits. Increasing the FRA has helped the government reduce the cost of the Social Security program, which paid out almost $870 billion to beneficiaries in 2015!*

While you can begin collecting benefits as early as age 62, the amount you receive as a monthly benefit will be less than it would be if you wait until you reach or surpass your FRA. It is important to note that if you file for your Social Security benefit before your FRA, **the reduction to your monthly benefit will remain in place for the rest of your life.** You can also delay receiving benefits up to age 70, in which case your benefits will be higher than your PIA for the rest of your life.

- At FRA, 100 percent of PIA is available as a monthly benefit.
- At age 62, your Social Security retirement benefits are available. For each month you take benefits prior to your FRA, however, the monthly amount of your benefit is reduced. *This reduction stays in place for the rest of your life.*
- At age 70, your monthly benefit reaches its maximum. After you turn age 70, your monthly benefit will no longer increase.

Year of birth	Full Retirement Age
1943-1954	66
1955	66 and 2 months
1956	66 and 4 months
1957	66 and 6 months
1958	66 and 8 months
1959	66 and 10 months
1960 or later	67**

---

* https://www.ssa.gov/news/press/basicfact.html
** http://www.ssa.gov/OACT/progdata/nra.html

ROLLING UP YOUR SOCIAL SECURITY

Your Social Security income "rolls up" the longer you wait to claim it. Your monthly benefit will continue to increase until you turn 70 years old. Even though Social Security is the foundation of most people's retirement, many Americans feel that they don't have control over how or when they receive their benefits. The truth is that every dollar you increase your Social Security income by means less money you will have to spend from your nest egg to meet your retirement income needs, but many retirees do not take advantage of this fact. For many people, creating their Social Security strategy is the most important decision they can make to positively impact their retirement. ***The difference between the best and worst Social Security decision can be tens of thousands of dollars over a lifetime of benefits.***

Deciding NOW or LATER: Following the above logic, it makes sense to wait as long as you can to begin receiving your Social Security benefit. However, the answer isn't always that simple. Not everyone has the option of waiting. Many people need to rely on Social Security on day one of their retirement. Some might need the income. Others might be in poor health and don't feel they will live long enough to make waiting until their FRA worthwhile for themselves or their families. It is also possible, however, that the majority of folks taking an early benefit at age 62 are simply under-informed about Social Security. Perhaps they make this major decision based on rumors and emotion.

File Immediately if You:
- Find your job is unbearable.
- Are willing to sacrifice retirement income.
- Are not healthy and need a reliable source of income.

Consider Delaying Your Benefit if You:
- Want to maximize your retirement income.

- Want to increase retirement benefits for your spouse.
- Are still working and like it.
- Are healthy and willing / able to wait to file.

So if you decide to wait, how long should you wait? Lots of people can put it off for a few years, but not everyone can wait until they are 70 years old. Your individual circumstances may be able to help you determine when you should begin taking Social Security. If you do the math, you will quickly see that between ages 62 and 70, there are 96 months in which you can file for your Social Security benefit. If you take into account those 96 months and the 96 months your spouse could also file for Social Security, and the number of different strategies for structuring your benefit, you can easily end up with more than 20,000 different scenarios. It's safe to say this isn't the kind of math that most people can easily handle. Each month would result in a different benefit amount. The longer you wait, the higher your monthly benefit amount becomes. Each month you wait, however, is one less month that you receive a Social Security check.

The goal is to maximize your lifetime benefits. That may not always mean waiting until you can get the largest monthly payment. Taking the bigger picture into account, you want to find out how to get the most money out of Social Security over the number of years that you draw from it. Don't underestimate the power of optimizing your benefit: the difference between the BEST and WORST Social Security election can easily be worth thousands of dollars in lifetime benefits. ***The difference can be very substantial!***

If you know that every month you wait, your Social Security benefit goes up a little bit, and you also know that every month you wait, you receive one less benefit check, how do you determine where the sweet spot is that maximizes your benefits over your lifetime? Financial professionals have access to software that will calculate the best year and month for you to file for benefits based on your default life expectancy. You can further customize that information by estimating your life expectancy based on your health, habits and family history. If you can then create an income plan (we'll get into this later in the chapter) that helps you wait until the target date for you to file for Social Security, you can optimize your retirement income strategy to get the most out of your Social Security benefit. How can you calculate your life expectancy? Well, you don't know exactly how long you'll live, but you have a better idea than the government does. They rely on averages to make their calculations. ***You have much more personal information about your health, lifestyle and family history than they do.*** You can use that knowledge to game the system and beat all the other people who are making uninformed decisions by filing early for Social Security.

While you can and should educate yourself about how Social Security works, the reality is you don't need to know a lot of general information about Social Security in order to make choices about your retirement. What you do need to know is exactly ***what to do to maximize your benefit.*** Because knowing what you need to do has huge impacts on your retirement! For most Americans, Social Security is the foundation of income planning for retirement. Social Security benefits represent about 39 percent of the income of the elderly.* For many people, it can represent the largest portion of their retirement income. Not treating your Social Security benefit as an asset and investment tool can lead to sub-optimization of your largest source of retirement income.

Let's take a look at an example that shows the impact of working with a financial professional to optimize Social Security benefits:

---

* *http://www.socialsecurity.gov/pressoffice/basicfact.htm*

» *Jeff and Kim Kroner are a typical American couple who have worked their whole lives and saved when they could. Jeff is 60 years old, and Kim is 56 years old. They sat down with a financial professional who logged onto the Social Security website to look up their PIAs. Jeff's PIA is $1,900 and Kim's is $900.*

If the Kroners cash in at age 62 and begin taking retirement benefits from Social Security, they will receive an estimated $568,600 in lifetime benefits. That may seem like a lot, but if you divide that amount over 20 years, it averages out to around $28,400 per year. The Kroners are accustomed to a more significant annual income than that. To make up the difference, they will have to rely on alternative retirement income options. They will basically have to depend on a bigger nest egg to provide them with the income they need.

If they wait until their FRA, they will increase their lifetime benefits to an estimated $609,000. This option allows them to achieve their Primary Insurance Amount, which will provide them a $34,200 annual income.

After learning the Kroners' needs and using software to calculate the most optimal time to begin drawing benefits, the Kroners' financial professional determined that the best option for them drastically increases their potential lifetime benefits to $649,000!

*By using strategies that their financial professional recommended, they increased their potential lifetime benefits by as much as **$80,000**. There's no telling how much you could miss out on from your Social Security if you don't take time to create a strategy that calculates your maximum benefit. For the Kroners, the value of maximizing their benefits was the difference between night and day. While this may seem like a special case, it isn't uncommon to find benefit increases of this* *magnitude. You'll never know unless you take a look at your own options.*

Despite the importance of knowing when and how to take your Social Security benefit, many of today's retirees and pre-retirees may know little about the mechanics of Social Security and how they can maximize their benefit.

So, to whom should you turn for advice when making this complex decision? Before you pick up the phone and call Uncle Sam, you should know that the Social Security Administration (SSA) representatives are actually prohibited from giving you election advice! Plus, SSA representatives in general are trained to focus on monthly benefit amounts, not the lifetime income for a family.

MAXIMIZING YOUR LIFETIME BENEFIT

As discussed in Chapter 2, calculating how to maximize **lifetime benefits** is more important than waiting until age 70 for your maximum **monthly benefit amount.** It's about getting the most income during your lifetime. Professional benefit maximization software can target the year and month that it is most beneficial for you to file based on your life expectancy.

The three most common ages that people associate with retirement benefits are 62 (Earliest Eligible Age), 66 (Full Retirement Age), and 70 (age at which monthly maximum benefit is reached). In almost all circumstances, however, none of those three most common ages will give you the maximum lifetime benefit.

Remember, every month you wait to file, the amount of your benefit check goes up, but you also get one less check. You don't know how exactly how long you're going to live, but you have a better idea of your life expectancy than the actuaries at the Social Security Administration who can only work with averages. They can't make calculations based on your specific situation. A professional can run the numbers for you and get the target date that maximizes your potential lifetime benefits. You can't get this information from the SSA, but you *can* get it from a financial professional.

Types of Social Security Benefits:
- *Retired Worker Benefit.* This is the benefit with which most people are familiar. The Retired Worker Benefit is what most people are talking about when they refer to Social Security. It is your benefit based on your earnings and the amount that you have paid into the system over the span of your career.
- *Spousal Benefit.* This is available to the spouse of someone who is eligible for Retired Worker Benefits.
- *Survivorship Benefit.* When one spouse passes away, the survivor is able to receive the larger of the two benefit amounts.
- *Restricted Application.* A higher-earning spouse may be able to start collecting a spousal benefit on the lower-earning spouse's benefit while allowing his or her benefit to continue to grow. Due to the Bipartisan Budget Act of 2015, this option is only available to individuals who turned age 62 before January 1, 2016.

In November of 2015, the Bipartisan Budget Act of 2015 was passed, which will have a dramatic impact on the way many Americans plan for Social Security. As the largest change to Social Security since 2000, the Bipartisan Budget Act of 2015 eliminated an estimated $9.5 billion* of benefits to retirees and may

---

* *http://www.nasdaq.com/article/congress-planning-to-close-social-security-loopholes-cm536252*

limit some of the flexibility you previously had to structure your benefits.

In 2000, Congress passed the Senior Citizens Freedom to Work Act. The bill allowed retirees to suspend receiving benefits so they wouldn't be subject to additional taxation if they chose to return to work after they filed for Social Security. However, by doing so, the bill also unintentionally created several loopholes in claiming strategies: most notably, the Restricted Application for spousal benefits and "file and suspend" filing strategy. For most Americans, the Bipartisan Budget Act of 2015 closed these loopholes by eliminating "file and suspend" and the Restricted Application.

The new rules mandate that:
- If a primary worker is not currently receiving benefits, then their dependents (child, spouse) can no longer collect benefits based on the primary worker's earning record.
- If you file for benefits, then you are filing for *all* benefits to which you are entitled—not just the benefit type you choose.

It's important to remember that in spite of these immense changes, one thing stayed the same—filing for Social Security is one of the most important financial decisions you will make in your lifetime, and a financial professional can help ensure you make the right one.

THE DIVORCE FACTOR

How does a divorced spouse qualify for benefits? If you have gone through a divorce, it might affect the retirement benefit to which you are entitled.

In general, a person can receive benefits as a divorced spouse on a former spouse's Social Security record so long as the following conditions are met:

- the marriage lasted at least 10 years; and
- the person filing for divorce benefits is at least age 62, unmarried, and not entitled to a higher Social Security benefit on his or her own record.*

With all of the different options, strategies and benefits to choose from, you can see why filing for Social Security is more complicated than just mailing in the paperwork. Gathering the data and making yourself aware of all your different options isn't enough to know exactly what to do, however. On the one hand, you can knock yourself out trying to figure out which options are best for you and wondering if you made the best decision. On the other hand, you can work with a financial professional who uses customized software that takes all the variables of your specific situation into account and calculates your best option. You have tens of thousands of different options for filing for your Social Security benefit. If your spouse is a different age than you are, it nearly doubles the amount of options you have. This is far more complicated arithmetic than most people can do on their own. If you want a truly accurate understanding of when and how to file, you need someone who will ask you the right questions about your situation, someone who has access to specialized software that can crunch the numbers. The reality is that you need to work with a professional that can provide you with the sophisticated analysis of your situation that will help you make a truly informed decision.

Important Questions about Your Social Security Benefit:
- How can I maximize my lifetime benefit? By knowing when and how to file for Social Security. This usually means waiting until you have at least reached your Full

---

* http://www.ssa.gov/retire2/yourdivspouse.htm

Retirement Age. A professional has the experience and the tools to help determine when and how you can maximize your lifetime benefits.
- Who will provide reliable advice for making these decisions? Only a professional has the tools and experience to provide you reliable advice.
- Will the Social Security Administration provide me with the advice? The Social Security Administration cannot provide you with advice or strategies for claiming your benefit. They can give you information about your monthly benefit, but that's it. They also don't have the tools to tell you what your specific best option is. They can accurately answer how the system works, but they can't advise you on what decision to make as to how and when to file for benefits.

The Maximization Report that your financial professional will generate represents an invaluable resource for understanding how and when to file for your Social Security benefit. When you get your customized Social Security Maximization Report, you will not only know all the options available to you—but you will understand the financial implications of each choice. In addition to the analysis, you will also get a report that shows *exactly* at what age—including which month and year—you should trigger benefits and how you should apply. It also includes a variety of other time-specific recommendations, such as when to apply for Medicare or take Required Minimum Distributions from your qualified plans. A report means there is no need to wonder, or to try to figure out when to take action—the Social Security Maximization Report lays it all out for you in plain English.

CHAPTER 5 RECAP //
- To get the most out of your Social Security benefit, you need to file at the right time.
- Maximizing your Social Security benefit depends on *when* and *how* you file.
- It's not impossible for you to calculate when the opportune time would be to trigger your Social Security income. In fact, with the tools and advice of a financial professional, it's quite easy.
- Every dollar your Social Security income increases is less money you'll have to spend from your nest egg to supplement your income.
- A financial professional held to fiduciary standards of liability can help you determine when you should file for Social Security to get your Maximum Lifetime Benefit.

6
FILLING YOUR INCOME GAP

The moment that you stop working and start living off the money that you've set aside for retirement can be referred to as the Retirement Cliff. You've worked and earned money your whole life, but the day that you retire, that income comes to an end. That's the day that you have to have other assets that fill the gap. Social Security will fill in some, but you need to come up with something else. After you have calculated your Social Security benefit and have selected the year and month that will maximize your lifetime benefits, it's time to look at your other retirement assets, incomes and options that will reduce or eliminate the dropoff of the Retirement Cliff. You may have a pension, an IRA or Roth IRA, dividends from stock holdings, money from the sale of real estate, rental property, or other sources of income. What other sources of reliable income do you have?

If your monthly Social Security check and your other supplemental income leaves a shortfall in your *desired* income, how are you going to fix it? This shortfall is called the **Income Gap** and it needs to be filled in order to maintain your lifestyle into retirement. What do you know you have coming in every month?

- Will you be receiving a pension?
- Will your spouse be receiving a pension?
- Will you be receiving wages from a part time job?
- Will you be receiving benefits from Social Security?
- Do you have any other sources of reliable, guaranteed income?

The difference between your guaranteed sources of income during retirement and the amount of income you need is called the **Income Gap.**

If you have a known income gap that you need to fill, you want to know how to fill that income gap with the fewest dollars possible. You basically want to buy that income gap for the least amount of money possible. You don't want it to cost you too much, because you want to get the most out of your other assets, including planning for your future and planning for your legacy. You do that by maximizing your Social Security benefit, leveraging your additional income and looking at other investment tools that can help generate income for you. Your specific needs, of course, should be analyzed by a professional.

TAKING A HYBRID APPROACH TO YOUR INCOME NEEDS

You looked at Social Security strategies earlier, discovering you have some control over how and when you file. Those decisions can change the outcome of your benefit in your favor. Once you start drawing that income, it is safer and will provide you with a reliable source of income for the rest of your life. While there are many factors of Social Security that you can control, there are many that you cannot.

For example, you do not have the choice of putting more money into Social Security in order to get more out of it. If you could have the option to contribute more money toward Social Security in order to secure a guaranteed income, it would be a great way to create a Green Money asset that would enhance your retirement. Since that option isn't available, you may seek an investment tool that is similar to Social Security that provides you with a reliable income. It also has the potential to increase the value of your principal investment! This kind of win-win situation exists, and it's called an annuity.

Today, you probably have savings in a variety of assets that you acquired over the years. But you may not have taken time to examine them and assess how they will support your retirement.

It's not about whether the market goes up or down, but when it does. If it goes down at the wrong time for your five or 10 year retirement horizon, you could be in serious danger of losing some of your retirement income.

If you have assets that you would like to structure for retirement income, *an annuity may be the right choice for you.*

Ask yourself the following questions:
- How concerned are you about finding a secure financial vehicle to protect your savings?
- How concerned are you that there may be a better way to structure your savings?

If you are concerned about the best way to fill your income gap, an income annuity investment tool is likely a good option for you. Income annuities have many similar qualities to Social Security that give them the same look and feel as that reliable benefit check you get every month. Most importantly, an income annuity can be an efficient and profitable way to solve your income gap.

HOW ANNUITIES FIT INTO AN OVERALL INCOME PLAN

Annuities are popular and reliable investment tools that allow you to secure income during retirement. In its simplest form, an annuity is a way to invest your money that allows you to structure it for income. Annuities come in a variety of modes. Finding the right one for you will take a conversation with your financial professional. Be sure you fully understand the features, benefits and costs of any annuity you are considering before investing money.

Here is how they can work:

When you put your money into an annuity, you are essentially buying an investment product from an insurance company. It is a contract between you and the insurance company that provides the investment tool. Let's say you have saved $100,000 and need it to generate income to meet your needs above and beyond your Social Security and pension checks. You give the $100,000 to an insurance company, who in turn invests it to generate growth.

They usually select investments that have modest returns over long term horizons. In other words, they generally put it somewhere stable and predictable. Most commonly, they will invest it in a combination of bonds and treasuries that are safer and dependable ways to grow money. They use the money from the insurance products they sell to invest, use a portion of the returns to generate profits for themselves, and return a portion to clients in the form of payouts, claims, and structured income options.

One of the most attractive qualities of these types of annuities is something called annual reset. Annual reset is sometimes also referred to as a "ratcheting." Instead of taking on the risk that comes with putting money in a fluctuating market, you can offset that risk onto the insurance company. It works like this: If the market goes down, you don't suffer a loss. Instead, the insurance company absorbs it. But if the market goes up, you share with the insurance company some of the profit made on the gain. The amount of gain you get is called your annuity participation rate. Typically the insurer will cap the amount of gain you can realize at somewhere between 3 and 7 percent. If the market goes up 10 percent, you would realize a portion of that gain (whatever percentage you are capped at). This means you to never lose money on your investment, while always gaining a portion of the upswings. The measurement period of your annuity can be calculated monthly, weekly and even daily, but most annuities are measured annually. The level of the index when you buy and the index level one year later will determine the amount of loss or gain. You and the insurance company are betting that the market will generally go up over time.

WHAT IS AN INCOME RIDER?

When you use that $100,000 to buy a contract with an insurance company in the form of an annuity, you are pegging your money on an index. It could be the S&P 500, the Dow Jones Industrial Average or any number of indexes. To generate income from the annuity, you select something called an income rider. An income rider is a subset of an indexed annuity. Essentially, it is the amount of money from which the insurance company will pay you an income while you have your money in their annuity. Your income rider is a larger number than what your investment is actually worth, and if you select the income rider, it will increase in value over time, providing you with more income. As the insurance company holds your money and invests it, they generate a return on it that they use to pay you a regular monthly income based on a higher number. The insurance company has to outperform the amount that they pay you in order to make a profit.

Remember, insurance companies make long-term investments that provide them with predictable flows of money. They like to stabilize the amount of money that goes in and out of their doors instead of paying and receiving large unpredictable chunks at once. When you opt for an income rider, an insurance company can reliably predict how much money they will pay out to you over a set period of time. It's predictable, and they like that. They can base their business on those predictable numbers.

The following example shows just how helpful an indexed annuity option with an income rider can be for a retiree:

> » *Frank and Michelle are 62 years old and have decided to run the numbers to see what their retirement is going to look like. They know they currently need $6,000 per month to pay their bills and maintain their current lifestyle. They have also*

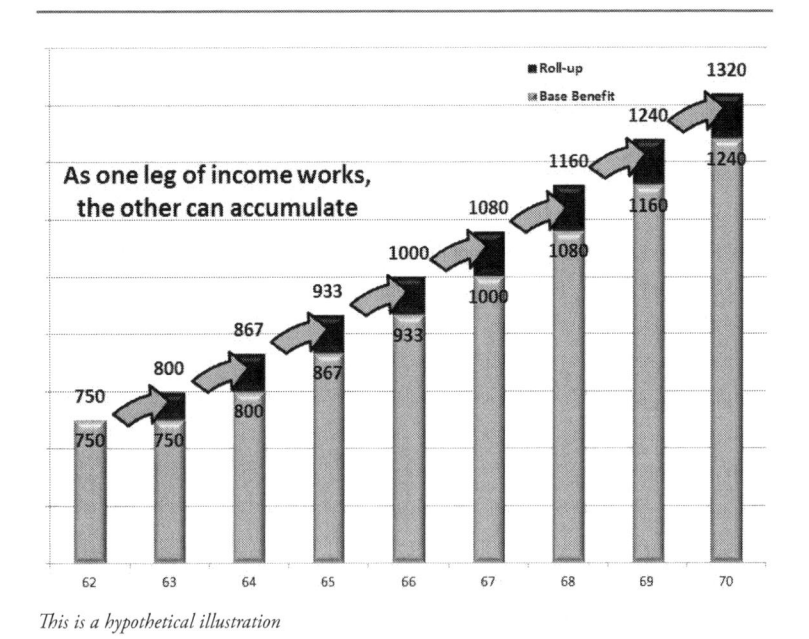

As one leg of income works, the other can accumulate

Age	62	63	64	65	66	67	68	69	70
Base Benefit	750	750	800	867	933	1000	1080	1160	1240
Roll-up	750	800	867	933	1000	1080	1160	1240	1320

This is a hypothetical illustration

done their Social Security homework and have determined that, between the two of them, they will receive $4,200 per month in benefits. They also receive $350 per month in rent from a tenant who lives in a small carriage house in their backyard. Between their Social Security and the monthly rent income, they will be short $1,450 per month.

They do have an additional asset, however. They have been contributing for years to an IRA that has reached a value of $350,000. They realize that they have to figure out how to turn the $350,000 in their IRA into $1,450 per month for the rest of their life. At first glance, it may seem like they will have plenty of money. With some quick calculations, they find they have 240 months, or nearly 20 years, of monthly income before they exhaust the account. When you consider income tax, the potential for higher taxes in the future, and market fluctuations (because many IRAs are invested in the market), the amount in the IRA seems to have a little less clout. Every dollar Frank and Michelle take out of the IRA is subject to income tax, and if they leave the remainder in the IRA, they run the risk of losing money in a volatile market. Once they retire and stop getting a paycheck every two weeks, they also stop contributing to their IRA. And when they aren't supplementing its growth with their own money, they are entirely dependent on market growth. That's a scary prospect. They could also withdraw the money from the IRA and put it in a savings account or CD, but removing all the money at once will put them in a tax bracket that will claim a huge portion of the value of the IRA. A seemingly straightforward asset has now become a complicated equation. Frank and Michelle didn't know what to do, so they met with their financial professional.

Their financial professional suggested that they use the money to purchase an indexed annuity with an income rider.

They selected an annuity that was designed for their specific situation. They took the lump sum from their IRA, placed it in an indexed annuity taking advantage of annual reset so they never lost the value of their investment. In return, they were guaranteed the $1,450 of income per month that they needed to meet their retirement goals. The simplicity of the contract allowed them to do an analysis with their professional just once to understand the product. They basically put their money in an investment crockpot where they didn't have to look at it or manage it. They just needed to let it simmer. In fact, their professional was able to find an annuity for them that allowed them their $1,450 monthly payment with a lump sum of $249,455, leaving them more than $100,000 to reinvest somewhere else. Keep in mind that annuities are tax deferred, meaning you will pay tax on the income you receive from an annuity in the year you receive it.

UNDERSTANDING SURRENDER CHARGES

In order to encourage investors to leave their money in their annuity contracts, insurance companies create surrender periods that protect their investments. If you remove your money from the annuity contract during the surrender period, you will pay a penalty and will not be able to receive your entire investment amount back. A typical surrender period is 10 years. If after three years you decide that you want your $100,000 back, the insurance company has that money tied up in bonds and other investments with the understanding that they will have it for another seven years. Because they will take a hit on removing the money from their investments prematurely, you will have to pay a surrender charge that makes up for their loss. During the surrender period, an annuity is not a demand deposit account like a savings or checking account. The higher returns that you are guaranteed from an annuity are dependent on the timeframe you selected.

The longer an insurance company can hold your money, the easier it is for them to guarantee a predictable return on it.

If you leave your money in the annuity contract, you get a reliable monthly income no matter what happens in the market. Once the surrender period has expired, you can remove your money whenever you want. Your money becomes liquid again because the insurance company has used it in an investment that fit the timeline of your surrender period. For many people, this is an attractive trade off that can provide a creative solution for filling their income gap.

When is an annuity with an income rider right for you? A good financial professional can help you make that determination by taking the time to listen closely to your situation and understanding what your needs are as you enter retirement. Every salesperson has a bag full of brochures and PowerPoint presentations, but they need to know exactly what the financial concerns of their individual clients are in order to help them make the most informed and beneficial decision. Some people need income today, others need it in five or 10 years. Others may have their income needs met but are planning to move closer to their children and will need to buy a house in 10 years. Or, if you want income in 15 years, you might want to choose a different investment product for 10 years, and then switch to an annuity with an income rider during the last five years of your timeline. Everyone's situation is different and everyone's needs are different. People who are interested in annuities, however, usually need to make decisions that affect their income needs, whether it is filling their income gap, or providing for income down the road.

What happens if you place on a shorter timeframe those assets from which you need to draw an income? Something called single premium immediate annuities may be for you:

SINGLE PREMIUM IMMEDIATE ANNUITIES (SPIA)
A single premium immediate annuity is simply a contract between you and an insurance company. SPIAs are structured so that you pay a lump sum of money (a single premium) to an insurance company, and they give you a guaranteed income over an agreed upon time period. That time period could be five years, or it could be for the remainder of your lifetime. Guarantees from insurance companies are based on the claims-paying ability of the issuing insurance company.

SPIAs provide investors with a stream of reliable income when they can't afford to take the risk of losing money in a fluctuating market. While there is general faith that the market always trends up, at least in the long-term, if you are focusing on income over a shorter period of time, you may not be able to take a big hit in the market. Beyond normal market volatility, interest rates also come with an inherent level of uncertainty, making it hard to create a dependable income on your own. SPIAs reduce risk for you by giving you regular monthly, quarterly or yearly payments that can begin the moment you buy the contract. Your financial professional can walk you through a series of different payment options to help you select the one that most closely fits your needs.

Additional Annuity Information:
- Some contracts will allow you to draw income from the high water mark that the market reaches each year. The income rider will then begin calculating its value from the high water mark.
- Variable annuities, however, can lose money with market fluctuations. As their name suggests, they vary with the market. These annuities do not take advantage of annual reset when the market goes down. The income rider will stay the same, but the value of your actual contract may fall. If you surrender the annuity, the insurance company

will pay you the market value of the asset, regardless of whether it matches, exceeds or falls short of the value at which you bought the contract. If its value has dropped significantly, you may be better off taking the income rider without surrendering your contract.
- Income annuities are investment tools that look and feel a bit like Social Security. Every year you allow the money to grow with the market, and it will "roll up" by a specific amount, paying out a specific percent to you as income each year.
- Annuities can work very well to create income, and a financial professional can help you find the one that best matches your income need, and can also structure it to work perfectly for you.

Managing Risk Within Your Annuity:
Just like any investment strategy, the amount of risk needs to fit the comfort level of the investor. Annuities are no exception. Without going into too much detail, here are some additional ways to manage risk with annuity options:
- If you want to structure an annuity investment for growth over a long period of time, you can select a variable annuity. The value of your principal investment follows the market and can lose or gain value with the market. This type of annuity can also have an income rider, but it is really more useful as an accumulation tool that bets on an improving market. A 40-year-old couple, for example, will probably want to structure more for growth and take on more risk than someone in their 70s. The 40-year-old couple may select a variable annuity with an income rider that kicks in when they plan to retire. If it rises with the market or outperforms it, the value of their investment has grown. If the market loses ground over the duration

of the contract or their annuity underperforms, they can still rely on the income rider.
- If you are 68 years old and you have more immediate income needs that you need to come up with above and beyond your Social Security, you need a low risk, reliable source of income. If you choose an annuity option, you are looking for something that will pay out an income right away over a relatively short timeframe. You probably want to opt for a SPIA that pays you immediately and spans a five year period, as well as an additional annuity that begins paying you in five years, and another longer term annuity that begins paying you in 10 years. Bear in mind that each annuity contract has its own costs and fees. Review these with your financial professional before you determine the best products and strategies for your situation.

The following story illustrates how using more than one kind of income annuity can be helpful for a retiree.

> *» Karen is 60 years old and is wondering how she can use her assets to provide her with a retirement income. She has a $5,000 per month income need. If she starts withdrawing her Social Security benefit in six years at age 66, it will provide her with $2,200 per month. She also has a pension that kicks in at age 70 that will give her another $1,320 per month.*
>
> *That leaves an income gap of $2,800 from ages 66 to 69, and then an income gap of $1,480 at age 70 and beyond. If Karen uses only Green Money to solve her income need, she will need to deposit $918,360 at 2 percent interest to meet her monthly goal for her lifetime. If she opts to use Red Money and withdraws the amount she needs each month from the market, let's say the S & P 500, she will run out of cash in*

10 years if she invested between the years of 2000 and 2012. Suffering a market downturn like that during the period for which she is relying on it for retirement income will change her life, and not for the better.

Working with a financial professional to find a better way, Karen found that she could take a hybrid approach to fill her income gap. Her professional recommended two different income vehicles: one that allowed her to deposit just $190,161 with a 2 percent return, and one that was a $146,000 income annuity. These tools filled her income gap with $336,161, requiring her to spend $582,000 less money to accomplish her goal! Working with a professional to find the right tools for her retirement needs saved Karen over half a million dollars.

CREATING AN INCOME PLAN

Creating an income plan before you retire allows you to satisfy your need for lifetime income and ensures that your lifestyle can last as long as you do. You also want to create a plan that operates in the most efficient way possible. Doing so will give more security to your Need Later Money and will potentially allow you to build your legacy down the road.

Here is a basic roadmap of what we have covered so far:

- Review your income needs and look specifically at the shortfall you may have during each year of your retirement based on your Social Security income, and income from any other assets you have.
- Ask yourself where you are in your distribution phase. Is retirement one year away? 10 years away? Last year?
- Determine how much money you need and how you need to structure your existing assets to provide for that need.

- If you have an asset from which you need to generate income, consider options offered by purchasing an income rider on an annuity.

CHAPTER 6 RECAP //
- Annuities are able to do what no other financial tool can do: they guarantee income. They function in a similar way to your Social Security benefit. Income annuities offer principal and income guarantees, and are considered a Green Money income asset.
- Although an annuity is an income-producing asset that does not subject your income to market risk, it still has the opportunity to grow. Indexed annuities participate in market-linked growth without market loss through a strategy known as indexing. Indexing combined with the power of annual reset gives you both growth and safety of your principal.
- When purchased with an income rider, the benefits of an income annuity include guarantee of principal, access to your money, a guaranteed lifetime income and money to your beneficiaries.
- Be sure you understand the features, benefits, costs and fees associated with any annuity product before you invest.

7
THE IMPACT OF MARKET VOLATILITY

Understanding your Social Security benefit, filling the income gap and making an overall plan that meets your retirement income needs is no small task. Once you have worked with a financial professional to structure your income needs, it's time to take a look at the future. With your immediate income needs met, you have the opportunity to take your additional assets and leverage them for profit to supplement your income in the future, to prepare for anticipated health care costs or to contribute to your legacy. Stable income also means that you should have the staying power to stick with your investment portfolio through the ups and downs in the market.

MATH OF REBOUNDS

A fickle market can raise the eyebrows of even the most veteran investor. Taking a hit in the market hurts no matter how stable your income. Part of the pain comes from knowing that when you take a step back in the market, it requires an even larger step forward to return to where you were. As the market goes up and down, those larger gains you need to realize to get back to zero start to look even more daunting.

HOW REAL PEOPLE MAKE INVESTMENT DECISIONS

It can be challenging to watch the stock market's erratic changes every month, week or even every day. When you have your money riding on it, the ride can feel pretty bumpy. When you are managing your money by yourself, emotions inevitably enter into the mix. The Dow Jones Industrial Average and the S&P 500 represent more to you than market fluctuations. They represent a portion of your retirement. It's hard not to be emotional about it.

Everyone knows you should buy low and sell high. But this is what is more likely to happen:

The market takes a downturn, similar to the 2008 crash, and investors see as much as a 30 percent loss in their stock holdings. It's hard to watch, and it's harder to bear the pain of losing that much money. The math of rebounds means that they will need to rely on even larger gains just to get back to where things were before the downturn. They sell. But eventually, and inevitably, the market begins to rise again. Maybe slowly, maybe with some moderate growth, but by the time the average investor notices an upward trend and wants to buy in again, they have already missed a great deal of the gains.

Emily's situation illustrates how market volatility can have major repercussions for an individual investor.

THE IMPACT OF MARKET VOLATILITY

» *Emily works for Acme Paper Company for 34 years. During her time there, she acquires bonuses and pay raises that often include shares of stock in the company. She also dedicates part of her paycheck every month to a 401(k) that bought Acme stock. By the time she retires, Emily has $250,000 worth of Acme stock.*

Although she had contributes to her 401(k) account every month, Emily doesn't cultivate any other assets that could generate income for her during retirement. Emily also retires early at age 62 because of her failing health. The commute to work every day was becoming difficult in her weakened condition and she wanted to enjoy the rest of her life in retirement instead of working at Acme.

Because she retires early, Emily fails to maximize her Social Security benefit. While she lives a modest lifestyle, her income needs will still be $3,500 per month. Emily's monthly Social Security check will only cover $1,900, leaving her with a $1,600 income gap. To supplement her Social Security check, Emily sells $1,600 of her Acme stock each month to meet her income needs. A $250,000 401(k) is nothing to sneeze at, but reducing its value by $1,600 every month will barely last Emily 10 years. And that's if the market stays neutral or grows modestly. If the market takes a downturn, the money that Emily relied on to fill her income gap will rapidly diminish. Even if the market starts going up in a couple of years, it will take much larger gains for her to recover the value that she lost.

Unhappily for Emily, she retired in 2007, just before the major market downturn that lasted for several years. She lost more than 20 percent of the value of her stock. Because Emily needed to sell her stock to meet her basic income needs, the market price of the stock was secondary to her need for the money. When she needed money, she was forced to sell *however many shares she needed to fill her income gap that month. And if she has a financial crisis, involving her need for medical care, for example, she will be forced to sell stock even if the market is low and her shares are nearly worthless. Emily realizes that she could have relied on an investment structured to deliver her a regular income while protecting the value of her investment. She could have kept her $250,000 from diminishing while enjoying her lifestyle into retirement regardless of the volatility of the market. Ideally, Emily would have restructured her 401(k) to reflect the level of risk that she was able to take. In her case, she would have had most of her money in Green Money assets, allowing her to rely on the value of her assets when she needed them.*

THE DALBAR STUDY

In 2013, DALBAR, the well-respected financial services market research firm, released their annual "Quantitative Analysis of Investment Behavior" report (QAIB). The report studied the impact of market volatility on individual investors: people like Lisa, or anyone who was managing (or mismanaging) their own investments in the stock market.

According to the study, volatility not only caused investors to make decisions based on their emotions, those decisions also harmed their investments and prevented them from realizing potential gains. So why do people meddle so much with their investments when the market is fluctuating? Part of the reason is that many people have financial obligations that they don't have control over. Significant expenses like house payments, the unexpected cost of replacing a broken-down car, and medical bills can put people in a position where they need money. If they need to sell investments to come up with that money, they don't have the luxury of selling when they *want* to. They must sell when they *need* to.

THE IMPACT OF MARKET VOLATILITY

DALBAR's "Quantitative Analysis of Investor Behavior" has been used to measure the effects of investors' buying, selling and mutual fund switching decisions since 1994. The QAIB shows time and time again over nearly a 20 year period that the average investor earns less, and in many cases, significantly less than the performance of mutual funds suggests. QAIB's goal is to improve independent investor performance and to help financial professionals provide helpful advice and investment strategies that address the concerns and behaviors of the average investor.

An excerpt from the report claims that:*

"QAIB offers guidance on how and where investor behaviors can be improved. No matter what the state of the mutual fund industry, boom or bust: Investment results are more dependent on investor behavior than on fund performance. Mutual fund investors who hold on to their investments are more successful than those who time the market.

QAIB uses data from the Investment Company Institute (ICI), Standard & Poor's and Barclays Capital Index Products to compare mutual fund investor returns to an appropriate set of benchmarks.

There are actually three primary causes for the chronic shortfall for both equity and fixed income investors:

1. *Capital not available to invest. This accounts for 25 percent to 35 percent of the shortfall.*
2. *Capital needed for other purposes. This accounts for 35 percent to 45 percent of the shortfall.*
3. *Psychological factors. These account for 45 percent to 55 percent of the shortfall."*

---

*2013 QAIB, Dalbar, March 2013

The key findings of Dalbar's QAIB report provide compelling statistics about how individual investment strategies produced negative outcomes for the majority of investors:
- Psychological factors account for 45 percent to 55 percent of the chronic investment return shortfall for both equity and fixed income investors.
- Asset allocation is designed to handle the investment decision-making for the investor, which can materially reduce the shortfall due to psychological factors.
- Successful asset allocation investing requires investors to act on two critical imperatives:
  1. Balance capital preservation and appreciation so that they are aligned with the investor's objective.
  2. Select a qualified allocator.
- The best way for an investor to determine their risk tolerance is to utilize a risk tolerance assessment. However, these assessments must be accessible and usable.
- Evaluating allocator quality requires analysis of the allocator's underlying investments, decision making process and whether or not past efforts have produced successful outcomes.
- Choosing a top allocator makes a significant difference in the investment results one will achieve.
- Mutual fund retention rates suggest that the average investor has not remained invested for long enough periods to derive the potential benefits of the investment markets.
- Retention rates for asset allocation funds exceed those of equity and fixed income funds by over a year.
- Investors' ability to correctly time the market is highly dependent on the direction of the market. Investors generally guess right more often in up markets. However, in 2012 investors guessed right only 42 percent of the time during a bull market.

THE IMPACT OF MARKET VOLATILITY

- Analysis of investor fund flows compared to market performance further supports the argument that investors are unsuccessful at timing the market. Market upswings rarely coincide with mutual fund inflows while market downturns do not coincide with mutual fund outflows.
- Average equity mutual fund investors gained 15.56 percent compared to a gain of 15.98 percent that just holding the S&P 500 produced.
- The shortfall in the long-term annualized return of the average mutual fund equity investor and the S&P 500 continued to decrease in 2012.
- The fixed-income investor experienced a return of 4.68 percent compared to an advance of 4.21 percent on the Barclays Aggregate Bond Index.
- The average fixed income investor has failed to keep up with inflation in nine out of the last 14 years.*

It doesn't take a financial services market research report to tell you that market volatility is out of your control. The report does prove, however, that before you experience market volatility, you should have an investment plan, and when the market is fluctuating, you should stand by your investment plan. You should also review and discuss your investment plan with your financial professional on a regular basis, ensuring he/she is aware of any changes in your goals, financial circumstances, your health or your risk tolerance. When the economy is under stress and the markets are volatile, investors can feel vulnerable. That vulnerability causes people to tinker with their portfolios in an attempt to outsmart the market. Financial professionals, however, don't try to time the market for their clients. They try to tap into the gains that can be realized by committing to long-term investment strategies.

---

*2013 QAIB, Dalbar, March 2013

CHAPTER 7 RECAP //

- The timing of market downturns is more critical to retirees than to the average investor. If you are making withdrawals on a market investment without first protecting your income, and the account suffers a loss, rapid depletion of your funds will change what the future of your retirement looks like.
- Emotions inevitably enter the mix during stock market downturns. According to the DALBAR "Quantitative Analysis of Investment Behavior" report released in 2013, the average fixed income investor managing their money alone failed to keep up with inflation in nine out of the last 14 years.

8
WHY YOU SHOULD CONSIDER MANAGED MONEY

Now that you've calculated the Rule of 100, determined how much risk you have and how much you want, and you've determined how much Green Money you need to meet your short-term and mid-term income needs, it's time to look at what you have left. The money you have left after you've calculated your Green Money needs has the potential of becoming Red Money: your stocks, mutual funds and other investment products that you want to continue accumulating value with the market. You now have the luxury of taking a closer second look at your Red Money to determine how you would like to manage it.

As you read earlier in the key findings of the DALBAR report, the deck is stacked against the individual investor. Remember that the average investor on a fixed income failed to keep pace with inflation in nine of the last 14 years, meaning the inherent risk in managing your Red Money is very real and could have a lasting impact on your assets. So, how much of your Red Money do you invest, and in what kinds of markets, investment products and stocks do you invest? There are a lot of different directions in which you can take your Red Money. One thing is for sure: significant accumulation depends on investing in the market. How you go about doing it is different for everyone. Gathering stocks, bonds and investment funds together in a portfolio without a cohesive strategy behind them could cause you to miss out on the benefits of a more thoughtful and planful approach. The end result is that you may never really understand what your money is doing, where and how it is really invested, and which investment principles are behind the investment products you hold. While you may have goals for each individual piece of your portfolio, it is likely that you don't have a comprehensive plan for your Red Money, which may mean that *you are taking on more risk than you would like, and are getting less return for it than is possible.*

Enter **Managed Money.**

MANAGED MONEY FOR LONG-TERM GROWTH

Managed Money is money that is managed by a professional *with a purpose*. After your income needs are met and you have assets that you would like to dedicate to accumulation, there are decisions you need to make about how to invest those assets. You can buy stocks, index funds, mutual funds, bonds—you name it—you can invest in it. However, the difference between Red Money and Managed Money is that Managed Money has a cohesive strategy behind it that is *implemented by a professional*. When you manage your Red Money with an investment plan, it becomes Managed Money: *money that is being managed with a specific purpose, a specific set of focused goals and a specific strategy in mind.* Managed Money is still a type of Red Money. It comes with different levels of risk. But Managed Money is under the watchful eye of professionals who have a stake in the success of your money in the market and who can recommend a range of strategies from those designed for preservation to those targeting rapid growth. You don't want to miss out on achieving the right level of risk, and more importantly, composing a careful plan for the return of your assets.

It can be helpful to think of Red Money and Managed Money with this analogy:

If you needed to travel through an unfamiliar city in a foreign country, you could rent a car or perhaps hire a driver. Were you to drive yourself, you would try to gain guidance from perplexing road signs and need to adhere to traffic rules—with no experience or assistance to lean on. It would take longer to get to where you want to go, and the chance of a traffic accident would be higher. If you hired a driver, they would manage your journey. A driver would know the route, how to avoid traffic, and follow the rules of the road.

Red Money is like driving yourself. With Managed Money, you are still traveling by car, but now you have a professional working on your behalf.

TAKING A CLOSER LOOK AT YOUR PORTFOLIO

Think about your investment portfolio. Think specifically of what you would consider your Red Money. Do you know what is there? You may have several different investment products like individual mutual funds, bond accounts, stocks, etc. You may have inherited a stock portfolio from a relative, or you might be invested in a bond account offered by the company for which you worked due to your familiarity with them. While you may or may not be managing your investments individually, the reality is that you probably don't have an overall management strategy for all of your investments. Investments that aren't managed are simply Red Money, or money that is at risk in the market.

Harnessing the earning potential of your Red Money relies on more than a collection of stocks and bonds, however. It needs guided management. A good Managed Money manager uses the knowledge they have about the level of risk with which you are comfortable, what you need or want to use your money for, when you want or need it and how you want to use it. The Managed Money objects that they choose for you will still have a certain level of risk, but under the right management, control and process, you have a far better chance of a successful outcome that meets your specific needs.

When you sit down with an investment professional, you can look at all of your assets together. Chances are that you have accumulated a number of different assets over the last 20, 30 or 50 years. You may have a 401(k), an IRA, a Roth IRA, an account of self-directed stocks, a brokerage account, etc. Wherever you put your money, a financial professional will go through your assets and help you determine the level of risk to which you are exposed now and should be exposed in the future.

Here is a typical example of how an investment professional can be helpful to a future retiree with Managed Money needs:

> » *Wendy is 65 years old and wants to retire in two years. She has a 401(k) from her job to which she has contributed for 26 years. She also has some stocks that her late husband managed. Wendy also has $55,000 in a mutual fund that her sister recommended to her five years ago and $30,000 in another mutual fund that she heard about at work. She takes a look at her assets one day and decides that she doesn't understand what they add up to or what kind of retirement*

they will provide. She decides to meet with an investment professional. Wendy's professional immediately asks her:

1. Does she know exactly where all of her money is? Wendy doesn't know much about all her husband's stocks, which have now become hers. Their value is at $100,000 invested in three large cap companies. Wendy is unsure of the companies and whether she should hold or sell them.

2. Does she know what types of assets she owns? Yes and no. She knows she had a 401(k) and IRAs, but she is unfamiliar with her husband's self-directed stock portfolio or the type of mutual funds she owns. Furthermore she is unclear as to how to manage the holdings as she nears retirement.

3. Does she know the strategies behind each one of the investment products she owns? While Wendy knows she had a 401(k), an IRA and mutual fund holdings, she doesn't know how her 401(k) is organized or how to make it more conservative as she nears retirement. She is unsure whether her IRA is a Roth or traditional variety and how to draw income from them? She really does not have specific investment principles guiding her investment decisions, and she doesn't know anything about her husband's individual stocks. One major concern for Wendy is whether her family would be okay if she were not around?

After determining Wendy's assets, her financial professional prepares a consolidated report that lays out all of her assets for her to review. Her professional explains each one of them to her. Wendy discovers that although she is two years away from retiring, her 401(k) is organized with an amount of risk with which she is not comfortable. Sixty percent of her 401(k) is at risk, far off the mark if we abide by the Rule of 100. Wendy opts to be more conservative than the Rule of 100 suggests, as she will rely on her 401(k) for most of her immediate income needs after retirement. Wendy's professional also

> *points out several instances of overlap between her mutual funds. Wendy learns that while she is comfortable with one of her mutual funds, she does not agree with the management principles of the other. In the end, Wendy's professional helps her re-organize her 401(k) to secure her more Green Money for retirement income. Her professional also uses her mutual fund and her husband's stock assets to create a growth oriented investment plan that Wendy will rely on for Need Later Money in 15 years when she plans on relocating closer to her children and grandchildren. By creating an overall investment strategy, Wendy is able to meet her targeted goals in retirement. Wendy's financial professional worked closely with her and her tax professional to minimize the tax impact of any asset sales on Wendy's situation.*

Like Wendy, you may have several savings vehicles: a 401(k), an IRA to which you regularly contribute, some mutual funds to which you make monthly contributions, etc. But what is your *overall investment strategy?* Do you have one in place? Do you want one that will help you meet your retirement goals? Managed Money looks at *ALL* your accounts and all their different strategies to create a plan that helps them all work together. Your current investment situation may not reflect your wishes. As a matter of fact, it likely doesn't.

You may have a better understanding of your assets than Wendy did, but even someone with an investment strategy can benefit from having a financial professional review their portfolio:

> » *Thomas is 69 years old. He retired four years ago. He relied on income from an IRA for three years in order to increase his Social Security benefit. He also made significant investments in 36 different mutual funds. He chose to diversify among the funds by selecting a portion for growth, another for good*

dividends, another that focused on promising small cap companies and a final portion that work like index funds. All the money that Thomas had in mutual funds he considered Need Later Money that he wanted to rely on in his 80s. After the stock market took a hit in 2008, Thomas lost some confidence in his investments and decided to sit down with a financial professional to see if his portfolio was able to recover.

The professional Thomas met with was able to determine what goals he had in mind. Specifically, the financial professional determined what Thomas actually wanted and needed the money for, and when he needed it. His professional also looked inside each of the mutual funds and discovered several instances of overlap. While Thomas had created diversity in his portfolio by selecting funds focused on different goals, he didn't account for overlap in the companies in which the funds were invested. Out of the 36 funds, his professional found that 20 owned nearly identical stock. While most of the companies were good investments, the high instance of overlap did not contribute to the healthy investment diversity that Thomas wanted. Thomas's financial professional also provided him with a report that explained the concentration ratio of his holdings (noting how much of his portfolio was contained within the top 25 stock holdings), the percentage of his portfolio that each company in which he invested in represented (showing the percentage of net assets that each company made up as an overall position in his portfolio) and the portfolio date of his account (showing when the funds in his portfolio were last updated: as funds are required to report updates only twice per year, it was possible that some of his fund reports could be six months old).

Thomas's professional consolidated his assets into one investment management strategy. This allowed Thomas's investments to be managed by someone he trusted who knew *his specific investment goals and needs. Eliminating redundancy and overlap in his portfolio was easy to do but difficult to detect since Thomas had multiple funds with multiple brokerage firms. Thomas sat down with a professional to see if his mutual funds could perform well, and he left with a consolidated management plan and a money manager that understood him personally. That's Managed Money at its best.*

AVOIDING EMOTIONAL INVESTING

There's no way around it; people get emotional about their money. And for good reason. You've spent your life working for it, exchanging your time and talent for it, and making decisions about how to invest it, save it and make it grow. The maintenance of your lifestyle and your plans for retirement all depend on it. The best investment strategies, however, don't rely on emotions. One of Managed Money's greatest strengths lies in the fact that it is managed by someone who understands your needs and desires, but doesn't make decisions about your money under the influence of emotion.

A well-managed investment account meets your goals as a whole, not in individualized and piecemeal ways. Professional money managers do this by creating requirements for each type of investment in which they put your money. We'll call them "screens." Your money manager will run your holdings through the screens they have created to evaluate different types of investment strategies. A professionally managed account will only have holdings that meet the requirements laid out in the overall management plan that was designed to meet your investment goals. The holdings that don't make it through the screens, the ones that don't contribute to your investment goals, are sold and redistributed to investments that your financial professional has determined to be appropriate.

WHY YOU SHOULD CONSIDER MANAGED MONEY

Different screens apply to different Managed Money strategies. For example, if one of your goals is significant growth, which would require taking on more risk alongside the potential for more return, an investment professional would screen for companies that have high rates of revenue and sales growth, high earnings growth, rising profit margins, and innovative products. On the other hand, if you want your portfolio to be used for income, which would call for lower risk and less return, your professional would screen for dividend yield and sector diversification. *Every investor has a different goal, and every goal requires a customized strategy that uses quantitative screens.* A professional will create a portfolio that reflects your investment desires. If some of the current assets you own complement the strategies that your professional recommends, those will likely stay in your portfolio.

Screening your assets removes emotions from the equation. It removes attachment to underperforming or overly risky investments. Financial professionals aren't married to particular stocks or mutual funds for any reason. They go by the numbers and see your portfolio through a lens shaped by your retirement goals. Your professional understands your wants and needs, and creates an investment strategy that takes your life events and future plans into account. It's a planful approach, and it allows you to tap into the tools and resources of a professional who has built a career around successful investing. Managing money is a full-time job and is best left to a professional money manager.

Removing emotions from investing also allows you to be unaffected by the day-to-day volatility of the market. Your financial professional doesn't ask where the market is going to be in a year, three years or a month from now. If you look at the value of the stock market from the beginning of the twentieth century to today, it's going up. Despite the Great Depression, despite the 1987 crash, despite the 2008 market downturn, the market, as a whole, trends up. Remember the major market downturn in 2008 when the market lost 30 percent of its value? Not only did it completely recover, it has far exceeded its 2008 value. Emotional investing led countless people to sell low as the market went down, and buy the same shares back when the market started to recover. That's an expensive way to do business. While you can't afford to lose money that you need in two, three or five years, your Need Later Money has time to grow. The best way to do so is to use Managed Money.

CREATING AN INVESTMENT STRATEGY

Just like Janet and Charles, chances are that you can benefit from taking a more managed investment approach tailored to your goals. Managed Money is generally Need Later Money that you want to grow for needs you'll have in at least 10 years. You can work with your financial planner to create investments that meet your needs within different timeframes. You may need to rely on some of your Managed Money in 10, 15 or 20 years, whether for additional income, a large purchase you plan on making or a vacation. Whatever you want it for, you will need it down the road. A financial professional can help you rescale the risk of your assets as they grow, helping you lock in your profits and secure a source of income you can depend on later.

So what does a Managed Money account look like? Here's what it *doesn't* look like: a portfolio with 49 small cap mutual funds, a dozen individual stocks and an assortment of bond accounts. A brokerage account with a hodgepodge of investments, even if goal-oriented, is not a professionally managed account. It's still Red Money. Remember, Managed Money is a managed account that has an overarching investment philosophy. When you look at making investments that will perform to meet your future income needs, the burning question becomes: How much should you have in the market and how should it be invested? Working with a professional will help you determine how much risk you should take, how to balance your assets so they will meet your goals and how to plan for the big ticket items, like health care expenses, that may be in your future. Yes, Managed Money is exposed to risk, but by working with a professional, you can manage that risk in a productive way.

WHY MANAGED MONEY?

If you have met your immediate income needs for retirement, why bother with professionally managing your other assets? The money you have accumulated above and beyond your income needs probably has a greater purpose. It may be for your children or grandchildren. You may want to give money to a charity or organization that you admire. In short, you may want to craft your legacy. It would be advantageous to grow your assets in the best manner possible. A financial professional has built a career around managing money in profitable ways. They are experts under the supervision of the organization that they represent.

Turning to Managed Money also means that you don't have to burden yourself with the time commitment, the stress, and the cost of determining how to manage your money. Managed Money can help you better enjoy your retirement. Do you want to sit down in your home office every day and determine how to best allocate your assets, or do you want to be living your life while someone else manages your money for you? When the majority of your Red Money is managed with a specific purpose by a financial professional, you don't have to be worrying about which stocks to buy and sell today or tomorrow.

SEEKING FINANCIAL ADVICE: STOCK BROKERS VS. INVESTMENT ADVISOR REPRESENTATIVES

Investors basically have access to two types of advice in today's financial world: advice from stock brokers and advice given by investment advisors. Most investors, however, don't know the difference between types of advice and the people from whom they receive advice. Today, there are two primary types of advice offered to investors: advice given by a commission-based registered representative (brokers) and advice given by fee-based Investment Advisor Representatives. Unfortunately, many investors are not aware that a difference exists; nor have they been explained the distinction between the two types of advice. In a survey taken by TD Ameritrade, the top reasons investors choose to work with an independent registered investment advisor are:*

- Registered Investment Advisors are required, as fiduciaries, to offer advice that is in the best interest of clients
- More personalized service and competitive fee structure offered at a Registered Investment Advisor firm
- Dissatisfaction with full commission brokers

The truth is that there is a great deal of difference between stock brokers and investment advisor representatives. For starters, investment advisor representatives are obligated to act in an investor's best interests in every aspect of a financial relationship. Confusion continues to exist among investors struggling to find the best financial advice out there and the most credible sources of advice.

Here is some information to help clear up the confusion so you can find good advice from a professional you can trust:

- Investment advisor representatives have the fiduciary duty to act in a client's best interest at all times with every investment decision they make. Stock brokers and brokerage firms usually do not act as fiduciaries to their investors and are not obligated to make decisions that are entirely in the best interest of their customers. For example, if you

---

*2011 Advisor Sentiment Study, commissioned by TD AMERITRADE. TD Ameritrade, Inc.

decide you want to invest in precious metals, a stock broker would offer you a precious metals account from their firm. An Investment Advisor would find you a precious metals account that is the best fit for you based on the investment strategy of your portfolio.
- Investment advisors give their clients a Form ADV describing the methods that the professional uses to do business. An Investment Advisor also obtains client consent regarding any conflicts of interest that could exist with the business of the professional.
- Stock brokers and brokerage firms are not obligated to provide comparable types of disclosure to their customers.
- Whereas stock brokers and firms routinely earn large profits by trading as principal with customers, Investment Advisors cannot trade with clients as principal (except in very limited and specific circumstances).
- Investment Advisors charge a pre-negotiated fee with their clients in advance of any transactions. They cannot earn additional profits or commissions from their customers' investments without prior consent. Registered Investment Advisors are commonly paid an asset-based fee that aligns their interests with those of their clients. Brokerage firms and stock brokers, on the other hand, have much different payment agreements. Their revenues may increase regardless of the performance of their customers' assets.
- Unlike brokerage firms, where investment banking and underwriting are commonplace, Registered Investment Advisors must manage money in the best interests of their customers. Because Registered Investment Advisors charge set fees for their services, their focus is on their client. Brokerage firms may focus on other aspects of the firm that do not contribute to the improvement of their clients' assets.

- Unlike brokers, Registered Investment Advisors do not get commissions from fund or insurance companies for selling their investment products.

Just to drive home the point, here is what a fiduciary duty to a client means for a Registered Investment Advisor. Registered Investment Advisors must:*
- Always act in the best interest of their client and make investment decisions that reflect their goals.
- Identify and monitor securities that are illiquid.
- When appropriate, employ fair market valuation procedures.
- Observe procedures regarding the allocation of investment opportunities, including new issues and the aggregation of orders.
- Have policies regarding affiliated broker-dealers and maintenance of brokerage accounts.
- Disclose all conflicts of interest.
- Have policies on use of brokerage commissions for research.
- Have policies regarding directed brokerage, including step-out trades and payment for order flow.
- Abide by a code of ethics.

---

* *2011 Advisor Sentiment Study, commissioned by TD AMERITRADE. TD Ameritrade, Inc.*

CHAPTER 8 RECAP //

- Managed Money is money that is managed by a professional. It is still considered a type of Red Money, but the risk is managed. There is a dedicated direction, strategy and end goal in mind, which makes it less dangerous.
- Red Money is like driving yourself in unfamiliar territory. With Managed Money, you are still traveling by car, but now you have a professional driving on your behalf.
- Managed Money is managed without emotions. A financial professional qualified to manage money uses a specific criteria designed to fit your overall goals for long-term growth.

9
NEW IDEAS FOR INVESTING

In Chapter 1, we discussed how today's investment options require advice that is relevant to today. Traditional, outdated investment strategies are not only ineffective, they can be harmful to the average investor. One of the most traditional ways of thinking about investing is the risk versus reward trade-off. It goes something like this:

- Investment options that are considered safer carry less risk, but also offer the potential for less return.
- Riskier investment options carry the burden of volatility and a greater potential for loss, but they also offer a greater potential for large rewards.

Most professionals move their clients back and forth along this range, shifting between investments that are safer and investments that are structured for growth. Essentially, the old rules of investing dictate that you can either choose relative safety *or* return, but you can't have both.

Updated investment strategies work with the flexibility of liquidity to remake the rules. Here is how:

There are three dimensions that are inherent in any investment: *Liquidity, Safety,* and *Return.* You can maximize any two of these dimensions at the expense of the third. If you choose Safety and Liquidity, this is like keeping your assets in a checking account or savings account. This option delivers a lot of Safety and Liquidity, but at the expense of any Return. On the other hand, if you choose Liquidity and Return, meaning you have the potential for great return and can still reclaim your money whenever you choose, you will likely be exposed to a very high level of risk.

Understanding Liquidity can help you break the old Risk versus Safety trade-off. By identifying assets from which you don't require Liquidity, you can place yourself in a position to potentially profit from relatively safe investments that provide a higher than average rate of return.

Choosing Safety and Return over Liquidity can have significant impacts on the accumulation of your assets. In Jerry's case, the paradigm shift from earning and saving to leveraging assets was a costly one.

> » *Jerry is a corn and soybean farmer with 1,200 acres of land. He routinely retains somewhere between $40,000 and $80,000 in his checking and savings accounts. If a major piece of equipment fails and needs repair or replacement, Jerry will need the money available to pay for the equipment and carry on with farming. If the price of feed for his cattle goes up one year, he will need to compensate for the increased*

overhead to his farming operation. He isn't a particularly wealthy farmer, but he has little choice but to keep a portion of money on hand in case something comes up and he must access it quickly. Most of his capital is held in livestock in the pasture or crops in the ground tied up for six to eight months of the year. When a major financial need arises, Jerry can't just harvest 10 acres of soybeans and use them for payment. He needs to depend heavily on Liquidity in order to be a successful farmer.

Old habits die hard, however, and when Jerry finally hangs up his overalls and quits farming, he keeps his bank accounts flush with cash, just like in the old days. After selling the farm and the equipment, Jerry keeps a huge portion of the profits in Liquid investments because that's what he is familiar with. Unfortunately for Jerry, with his pile of money sitting in his checking account, he isn't even keeping pace with inflation. After all his hard work as a farmer, his money is losing value every day because he didn't shift to a paradigm of leveraging his assets to generate income and accumulate value.

Almost anything would be a better option for Jerry than clinging to Liquidity. He could have done something better to get either more return from his money or more safety, and at the very least would not have lost out to inflation.

As you can see, choosing Liquidity solely can be a costly option. The sooner you want your money back, the less you can leverage it for Safety or Return. If you have the option of putting your money in a long-term investment, you will be sacrificing Liquidity, but potentially gaining both Safety and Return. Rethinking your approach to money in this way can make a world of difference and can provide you with a structured way to generate income while allowing the value of your asset to grow over time.

EMERGENCIES AND OPPORTUNITIES: YOUR LIQUID FUNDS

Once we establish adequate income to meet your needs now, our attention then focuses on how we can provide other sources of income to turn on down the road. Because you don't need all of your money to provide income right away, you have an opportunity to invest some for growth and liquidity. **Addressing your liquidity needs allows you to prepare for emergencies and take advantage of growth opportunities.** This can help provide a hedge against inflation and the increased medical costs not covered by your insurance.

How much do you need in an emergency fund? To build an emergency fund, you want to set aside enough cash in savings or money market accounts to provide for three to six months of expenses. After your emergency fund is established, then we will look at our growth opportunities. Using a hybrid mixture of Green, Managed, and maybe even Red Money, you can create accounts for intermediate and long-term growth. Remember: when setting up a growth plan for long-term, the priority is always income first. Once your income needs are secured, we can then use the additional funds to create long-term growth. This is one strategy that can help ensure your money lasts as long as you do.

The question is, how much Liquidity do you *really* need? Think about it. If you haven't sat down and created an income plan for your income and long-term growth needs, your perceived need for Liquidity is a guess. You don't know how much cash you'll need to fill the income gap if you don't know the amount of your Social Security benefit of the total of your other income options. If you *have* determined your income need and have made a plan for filling your income gap, you can partition your assets based on when you will need them. With an income plan in place, *you can use new rules to enjoy both Safety and Return from your assets.*

CHAPTER 9 RECAP //

- The three aspects of any investment include liquidity, safety, and return. You can choose to maximize any two against the third.
- Choosing to maximize liquidity alone can be an expensive option because the sooner you need your money back, the less you can leverage it for safety and return. To plan for a successful retirement in today's economy requires a creative use of today's financial tools.
- Establishing a cash reserve fund is a vital component of balancing your liquidity needs and planning for Need Later funds.

10
BE PREPARED FOR TAXES

Taxes play a starring role in the theater of retirement planning. Everyone is familiar with taxes (you've been paying them your entire working life), but not everyone is familiar with how to make tax planning a part of their retirement strategy.

Taxes are taxes, right? You'll pay them before retirement and you'll pay them during retirement. What's the difference? The truth is that a planful approach to taxes can help you save money, protect your assets and ensure that your legacy remains intact.

How can a tax form do all that? The answer lies in planning. ***Tax planning*** and ***tax reporting*** are two very different things. Most people only *report* their taxes. March rolls around, people pull out their 1040s or use TurboTax to enter their income and taxable assets, and ship it off to Uncle Sam at the IRS. If you use a CPA to report your taxes, you are essentially paying them to record history. You have the option of being proactive with your taxes and to plan for your future by making smart, informed decisions about how taxes affect your overall financial plan. Working with a financial professional who, along with a CPA, makes recommendations about your finances to you, will keep you looking forward instead of in the rearview mirror as you enter retirement.

TAXES AND RETIREMENT

When you retire, you move from the earning and accumulation phase of your life into the asset distribution phase of your life. For most people, that means relying on Social Security, a 401(k), an IRA, or a pension. Wherever you have put your Green Money for retirement, you are going to start relying on it to provide you with the income that once came as a paycheck. Most of these distributions will be considered income by the IRS and will be taxed as such. There are exceptions to that (not all of your Social Security income is taxed, and income from Roth IRAs is not taxed), but for the most part, your distributions will be subject to income taxes.

Regarding assets that you have in an IRA or a 401(k) plan that uses an IRA, when you reach 70 ½ years of age, you will be required to draw a certain amount of money from your IRA as income each year. That amount depends on your age and the balance in your IRA. The amount that you are required to withdraw as income is called a Required Minimum Distribution (RMD). Why are you required to withdraw money from your own account? Chances are the money in that account has grown over time, and the government wants to collect taxes on that growth. If you have a large balance in an IRA, there's a chance your RMD could increase your income significantly enough to put you into a higher tax bracket, subjecting you to a higher tax rate.

Here's where tax planning can really begin to work strongly in your favor. In the distribution phase of your life, you have a predictable income based on your RMDs, your Social Security benefit and any other income-generating assets you may have. What really impacts you at this stage is how much of that money you keep in your pocket after taxes. Essentially, *you will make more money saving on taxes than you will by making more money.* If you can reduce your tax burden by 30, 20 or even 10 percent, you earn yourself that much more money by not paying it in taxes.

How do you save money on taxes? By having a plan. In this instance, a financial professional can work with the CPAs at their firm to create a **distribution plan** that minimizes your taxes and maximizes your annual net income.

BUILDING A TAX DIVERSIFIED PORTFOLIO

So far so good: avoid taxes, maximize your net annual income and have a plan for doing it. When people decide to leverage the experience and resources of a financial professional, they may not be thinking of how distribution planning and tax planning will benefit their portfolios. Often more exciting prospects like planning income annuities, investing in the market and structuring investments for growth rule the day. Taxes, however, play a crucial role in retirement planning. Achieving those tax goals requires knowledge of options, foresight and professional guidance.

Finding the path to a good tax plan isn't always a simple task. Every tax return you file is different from the one before it because things constantly change. Your expenses change. Planned or unplanned purchases occur. Health care costs, medical bills, an inheritance, property purchases, reaching an age where your RMD kicks in or travel, any number of things can affect how much income you report and how many deductions you take each year.

Preparing for the ever-changing landscape of your financial life requires a tax-diversified portfolio that can be leveraged to balance the incomes, expenditures and deductions that affect you

each year. A financial professional will work with you to answer questions like these:
- What does your tax landscape look like?
- Do you have a tax-diversified portfolio robust enough to adapt to your needs?
- Do you have a diversity of taxable and non-taxable income planned for your retirement?
- Will you be able to maximize your distributions to take advantage of your deductions when you retire?
- Is your portfolio strong enough and tax-diversified enough to adapt to an ever-changing (and usually increasing) tax code?

» When Darlene returns home after a week in the hospital recovering from a knee replacement, the 77-year-old calls her daughter, sister and brother to let them know she is home and feeling well. She also should have called her CPA. Darlene's medical expenses for the procedure, her hospital stay, her medications and the ongoing physical therapy she attended amount to more than $50,000.

Americans can deduct medical expenses that are more than 10 percent of their Adjusted Gross Income (AGI). Darlene's AGI is $60,000 the year of her knee replacement, meaning she is able to deduct $45,500 of her medical bills from her taxes that year.[1] Her AGI dictated that she could deduct more than 80 percent of her medical expenses that year. **Darlene didn't know this.**

Had she been working with a financial professional who regularly asked her about any changes in her life, her spending, or her expenses (expected or unexpected), Darlene could have saved thousands of dollars. Darlene can also file an amendment to her tax return to recoup the overpayment.

This scenario presumes permanent laws in effect subsequent to 12/31/16

This relatively simple example of how tax planning can save you money is just the tip of the iceberg. No one can be expected to know the entire U.S. tax code. But a professional who is working with a team of CPAs and financial professionals have an advantage over the average taxpayer who must start from square one on their own every year. Have you been taking advantage of all the deductions that are available to you?

PROACTIVE TAX PLANNING

The implications of proactive tax planning are far reaching, and are larger than many people realize. Remember, doing your taxes in January, February, March or April means you are writing a history book. Planning your taxes in October, November or December means that you are writing the story as it happens. You can look at all the factors that are at play and make decisions that will impact your tax return *before* you file it.

Realizing that tax planning is an aspect of financial planning is an important leap to make. When you incorporate tax planning into your financial planning strategy, it becomes part of the way you maximize your financial potential. Paying less in taxes means you keep more of your money. Simply put, the more money you keep, the more of it you can leverage as an asset. This kind of planning can affect you at any stage of your life. If you are 40 years old, are you contributing the maximum amount to your 401(k) plan? Are you contributing to a Roth IRA? Are you finding ways to structure the savings you are dedicating to your children's education? Do you have life insurance? Taxes and tax planning affects all of these investment tools. Having a relationship with a professional who works with a CPA can help you build a truly comprehensive financial plan that not only works with your investments, but also shapes your assets to find the most efficient ways to prepare for tax time. There may be years that you could benefit from higher distributions because of the tax bracket that you are in, or there could be years you would benefit from taking less. There may be years when you have a lot of deductions and years you have relatively few. **Adapting your distributions to work in concert with your available deductions** is at the heart of smart tax planning. Professional guidance can bring you to the next level of income distribution, allowing you to remain flexible enough to maximize your tax efficiency. And remember, saving money on taxes makes you more money than making money does.

What you have on paper is important: your assets, savings, investments, which are financial expression of your work and time. It's just as important to know how to get it off the paper in a way that keeps most of it in your pocket. Almost anything that involves financial planning also involves taxes. Annuities, investments, IRAs, 401(k)s, 403(b), and many other investment options will have tax implications. Life also has a way of throwing curveballs. Illness, expensive car repair or replacement, or *any event that has a financial impact on your life will likely have a corresponding tax implication* around which you should adapt your financial plan. Tax planning does just that.

One dollar can end up being less than 25 cents to your heirs.

> » *When Peter's father passed away, he discovered that he was the beneficiary of his father's $500,000 IRA. Peter has a wife and a family of four children, and he knew that his father had intended for a large portion of the IRA to go toward funding their college educations.*
>
> *After Peter's father's estate is distributed, Peter, who is 50 years old and whose two oldest sons are entering college, liquidates the IRA. By doing so, his taxable income for that year*

puts him in a 39.6 percent tax bracket, immediately reducing the value of the asset to $302,000. An additional 3.8 percent surtax on net investment income further diminishes the funds to $283,000. Liquidating the IRA in effect subjects much of Peter's regular income to the surtax, as well. At this point, Peter will be taxed at 43.4 percent.

Peter's state taxes are an additional 9 percent. Moreover, estate taxes on Peter's father's assets claim another 22 percent. By the time the IRS is through, Peter's income from the IRA will be taxed at 75 percent, leaving him with $125,000 of the original $500,000. While it would help contribute to the education of his children, it wouldn't come anywhere near completely paying for it, something the $500,000 could have easily done.

As the above example makes clear, leaving an asset to your beneficiaries can be more complicated than it may seem. In the case of a traditional IRA, after federal, estate and state taxes, the asset could literally diminish to as little as 25 percent of its value.

How does working with a professional help you make smarter tax decisions with your own finances? Any financial professional worth their salt will be working with a firm that has a team of trained tax professionals, including CPAs, who have an intimate knowledge of the tax code and how to adapt a financial plan to it.

Here's another example of how taxes have major implications on asset management:

» Mike and Tierney, a 62-year-old couple, begin working with a financial professional in October. After structuring their assets to reflect their risk tolerance and creating assets that would provide them Green Money income during retirement, they feel good about their situation. They make decisions that allow them to maximize their Social Security benefits, they

have plenty of options for filling their income gap, and have begun a safe yet ambitious Managed Money strategy with their professional. When their professional asks them about their tax plan, they tell him their CPA handled their taxes every year, and did a great job. Their professional says, "I don't mean who does your taxes, I mean, who does your tax planning?" Mike and Tierney aren't sure how to respond.

Their professional brings Mike and Tierney's financial plan to the firm's CPA and has her run a tax projection for them. A week later their professional calls them with a tax plan for the year that will save them more than $3,000 on their tax return. The couple is shocked. A simple piece of advice from the CPA based on the numbers revealed that if they paid their estimated taxes before the end of the year, they would be able to itemize it as a deduction, allowing them to save thousands of dollars.

This solution won't work for everyone, and it may not work for Mike and Tierney every year. That's not the point. By being proactive with their approach to taxes and using the resources made available by their financial professional, they were able to create a tax plan that saved them money.

MANAGED MONEY AND TAXES

There are also tax implications for the money that you have managed professionally. People with portions of their investment portfolio that are actively traded can particularly benefit from having a proactive tax strategy. Without going into too much detail, for tax purposes there are two kinds of investment money: qualified and non-qualified. Different investment strategies can have different effects on how you are taxed on your investments and the growth of your investments. Some are more beneficial for one kind of investment strategy over another. Determining how to plan for the taxation of non-qualified and qualified investments is fodder for holiday party discussions at accounting firms. While it may not be a stimulating topic for the average investor, you don't have to understand exactly how it works in order to benefit from it.

While there are many differences between qualified and non-qualified investments, the main difference is this: qualified plans are designed to give investors tax benefits by deferring taxation of their growth until they are withdrawn. Non-qualified investments are not eligible for these deferral benefits. As such, non-qualified investments are taxed whenever income is realized from them in the form of growth.

Actively and non-actively traded investments provide a simple example of how to position your investments for the best tax advantage. In an actively traded and managed portfolio, there is a high amount of buying and selling of stocks, bonds, funds, ETFs, etc. If that active portfolio of non-qualified investments does well and makes a 20 percent return one year and you are in the 39.6 percent tax bracket, your net gain from that portfolio is only about 12 percent (39.6 percent tax of the 20 percent gain is roughly 8 percent.) In a passive trading strategy, you can use a qualified investment tool, such as an IRA, to achieve 13, 14 or 15 percent growth (much lower than the actively traded portfolio), but still realize a higher net return because the growth of the qualified investment is not taxed until it is withdrawn.

Does this mean that you have to always rely on a buy and hold strategy in qualified investment tools? Not necessarily. The question is, if you have qualified and non-qualified investments, where do you want to position your actively traded and managed assets? Incorporating a planful approach to positioning your investments for more beneficial taxation can be done many ways, but let's consider one example. Keeping your actively managed investment strategies inside an IRA or some other qualified plan could allow you to realize the higher gains of those investments without paying tax on their growth every year. Your more passively managed funds could then be kept in taxable, non-qualified vehicles and methods, and because you aren't realizing income from them on an annual basis by frequently trading them, they grow sheltered from taxation.

If you are interested in taking advantage of tax strategies that maximize your net income, you need the attentive strategies, experience and knowledge of a professional who can give you options that position you for profit. At the end of the day, what's important to you as the consumer is how much you keep, your after-tax take home.

ESTATE TAXES

The government doesn't just tax your income from investments while you're alive. They will also dip into your legacy.

While estate taxes aren't as hot of a topic as they were a few years ago, they are still an issue of concern for many people with assets. While taxes may not apply on estates that are less than $5 million, certain states have estate taxes with much lower exclusion ratios. Some are as low as $600,000. Many people may have to pay a state estate tax. One strategy for avoiding those types of taxes is to move assets outside of your estate. That can include gifting them to family or friends, or putting them into an irrevocable trust. Life insurance is another option for protecting your legacy.

BE PREPARED FOR TAXES

CHAPTER 10 RECAP //

- When you report your taxes, you are paying to record history. When you *plan* your taxes with a financial professional, you are proactively finding the best options for your tax return.
- It's important to understand the tax repercussions when tapping into assets from a 401(k) or a traditional IRA for use an income source. Money that is considered qualified by the federal government must be taxed upon distribution.
- At the age of 70 ½, the federal government requires all IRA participants to take their RMD, or Required Minimum Distribution. Failure to take your RMD can cost you thousands of dollars in taxes and penalty fees.
- Taxes play an important role during your retirement. It's important that you understand your obligations, and the differences between tax-deferred and tax-advantaged advantaged accounts.
- You make more money by saving on taxes than you do by making more money. This simple concept becomes extremely valuable to people in retirement and those living on fixed incomes.

11
THE FUTURE OF U.S. TAXATION

Although the phrase "nothing is certain except for death and taxes" is most famously attributed to Benjamin Franklin, variations of this saying existed even before the country's first taxes were levied, and these words continue to ring true to this day. However, due to recent upheavals in the American financial landscape, this saying might need to be modified to, "nothing is certain except for death and *increasing* taxes."

In the past 10 years alone, the United States has confronted both a debt ceiling and a fiscal cliff, and the federal debt has continued to grow by unprecedented amounts. With the wellbeing of the economy in jeopardy, legislation regarding debt reduction and tax reform has become a hot button issue. Regardless of which legislation has been, or will be, thrown at the American public, the truth of the matter remains the same: the country's current tax revenues cannot cover its obligations.

If the government wants to keep the lights on, it's going to need more income, which not only means that you can count on being taxed, but also on being taxed at an increasing rate.

DEBT CEILING – CAUSE AND EFFECTS

Since 1960, the debt ceiling has been raised by Congress 78 times. Increasing the debt ceiling is needed because the government keeps maxing out its credit limit, which it has been reliant upon since the beginning of the Industrial Revolution. Essentially, each time the federal government reaches the end of its line of credit; Congress raises the debt ceiling to extend it. This type of poor money management behavior is nothing new for many Americans: many people overuse their credit cards and rack up an impressive amount of debt. However, most people do not have the ability to raise the credit limit on a card once they have maxed it out—unless they can show they have the ability to pay the balance back. The only way to pay a credit line back is by making more money than you're spending. In other words, responsibility and a balanced budget are critical components to repaying a debt.

The federal government keeps finding ways to increase its credit line without also finding ways to proportionally cut its spending. Although some spending cuts have been put in place, they are not large enough to be worthy adversaries of the current debt situation. Consequently, the continual increasing of the debt ceiling has raised more than just the ability of the federal government to go further into debt; it has also raised concerns and fears about the direction in which the economy is heading. As investors' worry about the impact that future investment valuations may have on their personal wealth grows progressively serious, the market continues to swing unpredictably.

The truth of the matter is that raising the debt ceiling is only one part of the equation required to address the country's debt problem—tax reform is the other. If the government wants to try to staunch the flow of its ever-rising debt, then it will need to make more money, and the only way the government makes money is by collecting taxes. Unfortunately, however, the government frequently collects less than it spends: in 2014, the government collected approximately $42 billion less per month than it was spending.*

DEBT AND EARNINGS

Currently, the national debt is increasing at an unprecedented rate, rising to levels never seen before and threatening serious harm to the economy. In October 2004, the national debt was $7.4 trillion**, and by October 2014 it had climbed to $17.9 trillion***, which means the national debt grew 241.9 percent during this 10-year time period or 8.4 percent annually compounded. Since that time, the national debt growth rate has receded significantly and the national gross domestic product (GDP) has increased: in 2014, the annual debt growth rate had fallen to 4.5 percent and the GDP was approximately $17.5 trillion, up from $12.3 trillion in 2004.

However, even in spite of this progress, the gravity of the situation remains severe. At the end of 2011, the national debt level was 95.3 percent of the GDP. Economists believe that a sustainable economy exists at a maximum level of approximately

---

Congressional Budget Office projected deficit baseline 2014 - 2024
** *CBO, An Update to the Budget and Economic Outlook: 2014 - 2024*
*** *US Department of the Treasury's Bureau of the Fiscal Service, www.treasurydirect. gov/NP/debt/current*

80 percent. In 2014, the U.S. national debt was 101.8 percent of the GDP.*

The significance of these two numbers lies within the contrast. The national debt is the amount that needs to be repaid; this can be thought of as the government's credit card balance. The GDP represents the market value of all goods and services produced within a country during a given period. In other words, the GDP represents the gross taxable income available to the government. If debts are increasing at a rate greater than the gross income available for taxation, then the only way to make up the difference is to increase the rate at which the gross income is being taxed.

Since 2011, the national deficit's growth rate has experienced a significant downward trend that is expected to continue throughout 2015. After 2015, however, it is predicted that the deficit will once again begin to increase at an unprecedented rate.** Even more concerning is that the disparity between growth in national debt and growth in GDP is projected to continue, which means the amount of money the federal government owes will far outpace its ability to repay it. As anyone who has struggled with debt can tell you, continually borrowing more money than you make can have potentially disastrous consequences.

The increasing disparity between the debt and GDP rates of growth is not the only disconcerting story: national revenue collection rates offer further cause for concern. Since 1970, the average collection of GDP for revenue was approximately 17.3 percent. In 2012, the collection rate was at 14.4 percent, and rose to above 17 percent in 2014. This increase can be explained by several different tax increases that took place in the intervening years, as well as the effects of recent ROTH conversion limitation removals.

Federal Reserve Bank of St Louis Economic Research
**CBO, An Update to the Budget and Economic Outlook: 2014 - 2024*

By 2020, it is predicted the revenue rate will rise to be approximately 19.2 percent. When this increase is related to current tax rates, it means that someone currently in the 39.6 percent tax bracket would be pushed into a 44 percent tax bracket. The reality of this projected increase means that additional tax increases are on the horizon, and it would appear that this is going to be a graduated process that may begin as early as 2015. Consequently, when the debt ceiling discussions begin again they may be accompanied by a plan to implement additional tax increases over a period of three to five years.

Unfortunately, analysis of the federal government's budget also shows that regardless of revenue collection rates and increased taxes, the deficit will most likely continue to increase, and without additional spending cuts to help bring the budget into balance, tax increases are likely to continue.

THE END OF AN ERA

From a historical point of view, taxes are extremely low. The last time the U.S. national debt was even close to the same percentage level of GDP as it is today was for several years after the end of World War II. The maximum tax rate at that point, and through the years from 1944 through 1963, averaged 90 percent. Compare that to the maximum rate of 39.6 percent today, and it becomes very clear that there is a disparity of extreme proportion.

Taxes during this historical period were at extreme levels for nearly 20 years, throughout and following this level of debt-to-GDP. A significant point to note about the difference at that time versus where we are today is the economic activity. The period of 1944 through 1963 was in the heart of both the Industrial Revolution and the birth of the baby-boom generation. Today, we are mired in extreme volatility with frequent periods of boom and bust accompanied by the beginning of the greatest retirement wave ever experienced within the U.S. economy.

To contrast these two time periods with respect to the recovery period is almost asinine, as the external pressures from globalization and domestic unfunded liabilities did not exist or were irrelevant factors during the prior period.

To add insult to injury, U.S. domestic unfunded liabilities were estimated to be about $84 trillion in 2012 and that number has only increased through the intervening years.* These liabilities exist outside of the annual budgetary debt discussed above and are due to items such as Social Security, Medicare and government pensions. The most concerning part of this stems from the fact that we are on the cusp of the greatest retirement wave in U.S. history as the baby-boom generation begins retiring and drawing from the unfunded Social Security for which they currently have entitlement. Over the long-run, expenditures related to healthcare programs such as Medicare and Medicaid are projected to grow faster than the economy overall as the population matures.

To put unfunded liabilities into perspective, consider these as off-balance-sheet obligations similar to those of Enron. Although these are not listed as part of the national debt, they must be paid just the same. The difference between Enron and the U.S. unfunded liabilities is that if the U.S. government cannot come up with the funds to pay all these liabilities through revenue generation then they will print the money necessary to pay the debt.

WHAT DOES THE SOLUTION LOOK LIKE?

Unfortunately, the general public is in a no-win situation for this solution to the problem. Printing money does not bode well for economic growth as this action creates inflationary pressures that devalue the U.S. dollar and make everyone less wealthy. Cutting the entitlements that compose this liability leaves millions

---

* *National Center for Policy Analysis, How Much Does the Federal Government Owe?, June 2012*

THE FUTURE OF U.S. TAXATION

of people without benefits they have come to expect. The only other option, and one that the government knows all too well, is increased taxes. In fact, according to a Congressional Budget Office paper issued in 2004*, unfunded liabilities are addressed as follows:

"The term 'unfunded liability' has been used to refer to a gap between the government's projected financial commitment under a particular program and the revenues that are expected to be available to fund that commitment. But no government obligation can be truly considered 'unfunded' because of the U.S. government's sovereign power to tax—which is the ultimate resource to meet its obligations."

A balanced budget is going to be required at some point and with this will come higher taxes. Given our current position and projected budgets, it is likely that tax increases are coming in the near future. However, although raising taxes is a strategy to raise money, it is not a solution to the government's current and pending fiscal problems.

How do you prepare? Why spend so much time reassuring you that taxes will increase? Because you have an opportunity to take action. Now is the time to prepare for what is to come by structuring countermeasures for the good, the bad, and the ugly of each of these legislative nightmares through tax-advantaged retirement planning.

The truth of the matter is that you make more money by saving on taxes than you do by making more money. The simplistic logic of this statement makes sense when you discover it takes a $1.50 in earnings to put that same dollar, saved in taxes, back in your pocket.** This simple concept becomes extremely valuable to people in retirement and those living on fixed incomes.

---

* *CBO paper, Measures of the U.S. Government's Fiscal Position Under Current Law, Sept. 2004*

** *Assuming a 33 percent effective tax rate*

As simple as it sounds, it is much more difficult to execute. Most people fail to put together a plan as they near retirement, beginning with a simple cash flow budget. If you have not analyzed your proposed income streams and expenses, you could not possibly have taken the time to position these cash flows and other events into a tax-preferred plan.

Most people will state, "I have a plan" and thus, they do not need any further assistance in this area. The truth in most instances is that many of these people could not show you their plan, and of the few that could, they would not be able to show you how they have executed it. In this regard, they may as well be Richard Nixon saying, "I am not a crook" for as much as they claim, "I have a plan." The truth lies in waiting.

As you approach or begin retirement, you should look at what cash flows you will have. Do you have a pension? How about Social Security? How much additional cash flow are you going to need to draw from your assets to maintain the lifestyle that you desire?

Most people spend their whole lives saving and accumulating wealth but very little time determining a strategy that will distribute this accumulation in ways that will help them to retain it. You need to make sure you have the appropriate diversification of taxable versus non-taxable assets to complement your distribution strategy.

THE BENEFITS OF DIVERSIFICATION

Heading into retirement, you should be situated within a diversified tax landscape. The point to spending your whole life accumulating wealth is not to see how big the number is on paper, but rather to be an exercise in how much you put in your pocket after removing it from the paper.

To truly understand tax diversification, you must understand what types of money exist and how each of these will be treated

during accumulation and, most importantly, during distribution. The following is a brief summary:
1. Free money
2. Tax-advantaged money
3. Tax-deferred money
4. Taxable money
    a. Ordinary income
    b. Capital gains and qualified dividends

FREE MONEY

Free money is the best kind of money regardless of the tax treatment, because in the end you have more money than you would have otherwise. Many employers will provide contributions toward employee retirement accounts to offer additional employment benefits and inspire employees to save for their own retirement. With this, employers often will offer a matching contribution in which they will contribute up to a certain percentage of an employee's salary, generally three to five percent, to that employee's retirement account when the employee contributes to their retirement account as well. For example, if an employee earns $50,000 annually and contributes three percent ($1,500) to their retirement account annually, the employer will also contribute three percent ($1,500) to the employee's account. That is $1,500 in free money. Take all that you can get!

TAX-ADVANTAGED MONEY

Tax-advantaged money is the next best thing to free-money. Although you have to earn tax-advantaged money you do not have to give part of it away to Uncle Sam. Tax-advantaged money comes in three basic forms that you can utilize during your lifetime; four if prison inspires your future, but it's not necessary to discuss that option.

One of the most commonly known forms of tax-advantaged money is municipal bonds, which earn and pay interest that could be federally tax-advantaged, state tax-advantaged, or both state and federal tax-advantaged. There are several caveats that should be discussed in regard to the notion of tax-advantaged income from municipal bonds. First, you will notice that tax-advantaged has several flavors from the state and federal perspective. This is because states will generally tax the interest earned on a municipal bond unless the bond is offered from an entity located within that state. This severely limits the availability of completely tax-advantaged municipal bonds and constrains underlying risk and liquidity factors. Second, municipal bond interest gets added back into the equation for determining your modified adjusted gross income (MAGI) for Social Security and could push your income above the thresholds subjecting a portion of your Social Security income to taxation. In effect, if this interest subjects some other income to taxation then this interest is truly being taxed. Last, municipal bond interest may be excluded from the regular federal tax system, but it is included for determining tax under the alternative minimum tax (AMT) system. In its basic form, the AMT system is a separate tax system that applies if the tax computed under AMT exceeds the tax computed under the regular tax system, the difference between these two computations is the alternative minimum tax.

TAX-FREE MONEY: ROTH IRA

Roth accounts are probably the single greatest tax asset that has come from Congress outside of life insurance and are well known but rarely used. Roth IRAs were first established by the Taxpayer Relief Act of 1997 and were named after Senator William Roth, the chief sponsor of the legislation. A Roth account is simply an account in the form of an individual retirement account or an employer-sponsored retirement account that allows for tax-advantaged growth of earnings and, thus, tax-advantaged income.

The main difference between a Roth and a traditional IRA or employer-sponsored plan lies within the timing of the taxation. You're probably very familiar with the typical scenario of putting money away for retirement through an employer plan, whereby your employer deducts money from each paycheck and puts it directly into a retirement account. This money is taken out before taxes are calculated meaning you do not pay tax on those earnings today. A Roth account, on the other hand, takes the money *after* the taxes have been taken out and then puts it into the retirement account, so you do pay tax on the money today. The other significant difference between these two is taxation during distribution in later years. With a traditional retirement account, when you take the money out later it gets added to your ordinary income and is taxed accordingly. Additionally, including this in your income subjects you to the consequences previously mentioned for municipal bonds with Social Security taxation, AMT, as well as higher Medicare premiums. A Roth, on the other hand, has tax-advantaged distributions and does not contribute toward negative impact items such as Social Security taxation, AMT, or Medicare premium increases. It essentially comes back to you without tax and other obligations.

The best way to consider the difference between the two accounts is to look at the life of a farmer. A farmer will buy seed, plant it in the ground, grow the crops, and harvest it later for sale. Typically, the farmer would only pay tax on the crops that have been harvested and sold. But if you were the farmer, would you rather pay tax on $5,000 worth of seed that you plant today or $50,000 worth of harvested crop later? The obvious answer is $5,000 worth of seed today. The truth of the matter is that you are a farmer, except you are planting dollars into your retirement account instead of seeds into the earth.

So why doesn't everyone have a Roth retirement account if things are so simple? There are several reasons, but the single greatest reason has been the constraints on contributions. If you earned over certain thresholds (MAGI over $129,000 single and $191,000 joint for 2014), you were not eligible to make contributions, and, until 2010, if your modified adjusted gross income (MAGI) was over $100,000 (single or joint) then you could not convert a traditional IRA to a Roth. Outside of these contribution limits, most people save for retirement through their employers and most employers are not offering Roth options within their plans. The reason behind this is because Roth accounts are not that well understood and people have been educated to believe that saving on taxes today is the best possible course of action.

TAX-FREE MONEY: LIFE INSURANCE

As previously mentioned, the single greatest tax asset that has come from Congress outside of life insurance is the Roth account. Life insurance is the little known or discussed tax asset that holds some of the greatest value for your financial history both during life and upon death, and it is by far the best tax-advantaged device available. Traditionally, life insurance is viewed as a way to protect your loved ones from financial ruin upon your demise and it should be noted that everyone who cares about someone should have life insurance. By purchasing a life insurance policy, your loved ones will be assured a financial windfall from the life insurance company when you die that will help them with your final expenses and carry on their lives without you comfortably. The best part about the life insurance windfall is the fact that nobody will have to pay tax on the money received. This is the single greatest tax-advantaged device available, but it has one downside, you do not get to use it. Only your heirs will.

The little known and discussed part of life insurance is the cash value build-up within whole life and universal life (permanent) policies. Life insurance is not typically seen as an investment vehicle for building wealth and retirement planning, although it should briefly be discussed why this thought process should be reevaluated. Permanent life insurance is generally misconceived as something that is very expensive for a wealth accumulation vehicle as there are mortality charges (fees for the death benefit) that detract from the returns that are available and further, those returns do not yield as much as the stock market over the long run. This is why many times you will hear the phrase "buy term and invest the rest," where "term" refers to term insurance.

It's important to review the two terms just used in regard to life insurance: term and permanent. Term insurance is what most people are familiar with. You purchase a certain death benefit that will go to your heirs upon your death and this policy will be in effect for a certain number of years, typically 10 to 20 years. The 10 to 20 years is the term of the policy and once you have reached that end you no longer have insurance unless you purchase another policy at that point.

On the other hand, permanent insurance has no term involved, it is permanent as long as the premiums continue to be paid. Permanent insurance generally has higher premiums than term insurance for the same amount of death benefit coverage and it is this difference that is referred to when people say "invest the rest."

Simply speaking, there are significant differences between these two policies that do not get taken into consideration when providing a comparative analysis in the numbers. One item that gets lost in the fray when comparing term and permanent insurance is that term usually expires before death, in fact insurance studies show less than 1 percent of all term policies pay out death benefit claims. The issue arises when the term expires and the desire to have more insurance is still present. A term policy with the same benefit will be much more expensive than the original policy and, many times, life events occur, such as cancer or heart conditions, which makes it impossible to acquire another policy and leaves your loved ones unprotected and tax-advantaged legacy planning out of the equation.

Another aspect and probably the most important piece in consideration of the future of taxation is the fact that permanent insurance has a cash accumulation value. Two aspects stand out with the cash accumulation value. First, as the cash accumulation value increases the death benefit will also increase whereas term insurance is level. Second, this cash accumulation offers value to you during your lifetime rather than just your heirs upon death. The cash accumulation value can be used for tax-advantaged income during your lifetime through policy loans. Most importantly, this tax-advantaged income is available during retirement for distribution planning, all while offering the same typical financial protection to your heirs.

TAX-DEFERRED MONEY

Tax-deferred money is the type of money from which most people are familiar, but the idea was also briefly reviewed above. Tax-deferred money is typically your traditional IRA, employer sponsored retirement plan, or a non-qualified annuity. Essentially, money is put into an investment vehicle that will accumulate in value over time and you do not pay taxes on the earnings that grow in these accounts until it is distributed. Taxes must be paid once the money is distributed and, in addition to the taxes, the same negative consequences exist toward additional taxation and expense in other areas as previously discussed.

TAXABLE MONEY

Taxable money is everything else and is taxable both today and later, whenever it is received.

Of these four types of money, they really come down to two distinct classifications: taxable and tax-advantaged.

The greatest difference when comparing taxable and tax-advantaged income is a function of how much money you will keep after tax. For help in determining what the differences should be, excluding outside factors such as Social Security taxation and AMT, a tax equivalent yield should be used.

TAX-FREE IN THE REAL WORLD
To put the tax equivalent yield into perspective, consider the following example:

Bob and Mary are currently retired and in the 25 percent tax bracket living on Social Security and interest from investments. They have a substantial portion of their investments in municipal bonds yielding 6.0 percent, which in today's market is quite comforting. The tax equivalent yield they would need to earn from a taxable investment would be 8.0 percent, a 2.0 percent gap which seems almost impossible given current market volatility. However, something that has never been put into perspective is that the interest from their municipal bonds is subject to taxation on their Social Security benefits* (at 21.25 percent). With this, the yield on their municipal bonds would be 4.725 percent**, and the taxable equivalent yield falls to 6.3 percent leaving a gap of only 1.575 percent.

In the end, most people spend their lives accumulating wealth through the best, if not only vehicle they know, a tax-deferred account. This account is most likely a 401(k) or 403(b) plan offered through your employer and may be supplemented with an IRA that was established at one point or another. As the years go by, people blindly throw money into these accounts in an effort to save for a retirement that they someday hope to reach.

Assuming each dollar of interest subjects a dollar of Social Security income to taxation at 85 percent

**6.0 percent – (6.0 percent -21.25 percent) = 4.725 percent*

The truth is most people have an age selected for when they would like to retire but spend their lives wondering if they will ever be able to actually quit working. To answer this question, you must understand how much money you will have available to contribute toward your needs. In other words, you need to know what your after-tax income will be during this period.

All else being equal, it would not matter if you put your money into a taxable, tax-deferred, or tax-advantaged account as long as income tax rates never change and outside factors are never an event. The net amount you receive in the end will be the same. Unfortunately, this will never be the case. We already know that taxes will increase in the future, meaning we will likely see higher taxes in retirement than during our peak earning years.

Regardless, saving for retirement in any form is a good thing since it appears from all practical perspectives that future government benefits will be cut and taxes will increase. You have the ability to plan today for efficient tax diversification and maximization of your after-tax dollars during your distribution years.

CHAPTER 11 RECAP //

- The future of U.S. taxation is uncertain. You know what the tax rate and landscape is today, but you won't tomorrow. The only thing you can really count on is the trend of increasing taxation.
- Most people are familiar with tax-deferred methods of retirement savings such a traditional IRAs. By taking action now, you can prepare for the rise in taxes by restructuring your assets to include the benefits of tax-advantaged money.
- Tax-advantaged money is money you earn without having to pay taxes on it. One of the most common forms includes municipal bonds, but be aware these come with many state and federal caveats and complexities.
- Roth IRAs and life insurance are two forms of tax-advantaged money that can take advantage of today's lower tax rate when preparing for tomorrow's retirement.

12
THE BRANDEIS STORY

Louis Brandeis provides one of the best examples illustrating how tax planning works. Brandeis was Associate Justice on the Supreme Court of the United States from 1916 to 1939. Born in Louisville, Kentucky, Brandeis was an intelligent man with a touch of country charm. He described tax planning this way:

"*I live in Alexandria, Virginia. Near the Court Chambers, there is a toll bridge across the Potomac. When in a rush, I pay the dollar toll and get home early. However, I usually drive outside the downtown section of the city and cross the Potomac on a free bridge.*

The bridge was placed outside the downtown Washington, D.C. area to serve a useful social service—getting drivers to drive the extra mile and help alleviate congestion during the rush hour.

If I went over the toll bridge and through the barrier without paying a toll, I would be committing tax evasion.

If I drive the extra mile and drive outside the city of Washington to the free bridge, I am using a legitimate, logical and suitable method of tax avoidance, and I am performing a useful social service by doing so.

*The tragedy is that **few people know that the free bridge exists.**"*

Like Brandeis, most American taxpayers have options when it comes to "crossing the Potomac," so to speak. It's a financial planner's job to tell you what options are available. You can wait until March to file your taxes, at which time you might pay someone to report and pay the government a larger portion of your income. However, you could instead file before the end of the year, work with your financial professional and incorporate a tax plan as part of your overall financial planning strategy. Filing later is like crossing the toll bridge. Tax planning is like crossing the free bridge.

Which would you rather do?

The answer to this question is easy. Most people want to save money and pay less in taxes. What makes this situation really difficult in real life, however, is that the signs along the side of the road that direct us to the free bridge are not that clear. To normal Americans, and to plenty of people who have studied it, the U.S. tax code is easy to get lost in. There are all kinds of rules, exceptions to rules, caveats and conditions that are difficult to understand, or even to know about. What you really need to know is your options and the bottom line impacts of those options.

ROTH IRA CONVERSIONS

The attractive qualities of Roth IRAs may have prompted you to explore the possibility of moving some of your assets into a Roth account. Another important difference between the accounts is how they treat Required Minimum Distributions (RMDs). When you turn 70 ½ years old, you are required to take a minimum amount of money out of a traditional IRA. This amount is your

RMD. It is treated as taxable income. Roth IRAs, however, do not have RMDs, and their distributions are not taxable. Quite a deal, right?

While having a Roth IRA as part of your portfolio is a good idea, converting assets to a Roth IRA can pose some challenges, depending on what kinds of assets you want to transfer.

One common option is the conversion of a traditional IRA to a Roth IRA. You may have heard about converting your IRA to a Roth IRA, but you might not know the full net result on your income. The main difference between the two accounts is that the growth of investments within a traditional IRA is not taxed until income is withdrawn from the account, whereas taxes are charged on contribution amounts to a Roth IRA, not withdrawals. The problem, however, is that when assets are removed from a traditional IRA, even if the assets are being transferred to a Roth IRA account, taxes apply.

There are a lot of reasons to look at Roth conversions. People have a lot of money in IRAs, up to multiple millions of dollars. Even with $500,000, when they turn 70 ½ years old, their RMD is going to be approximately $18,000, and they have to take that out whether they want to or not. It's a tax issue. Essentially, if you will be subject to high RMDs, it could have impacts on how much of your Social Security is taxable, and on your tax bracket.

By paying taxes now instead of later on assets in a Roth IRA, you can realize tax-advantaged growth. You pay once and you're done paying. Your heirs are done paying. It's a powerful tool. Here's a simple example to show you how powerful it can be:

Imagine that you pay to convert a traditional IRA to a Roth. You have decided that you want to put the money in a vehicle that gives you a tax-advantaged income option down the road. If you pay a 25 percent tax on that conversion and the Roth IRA then doubles in value over the next 10 years, you could look at your situation as only having paid 12.5 percent tax.

The prospect of tax-advantaged income is a tempting one. While you have to pay a conversion tax to transfer your assets, you also have turned taxable income into tax free retirement money that you can let grow as long as you want without being required to withdraw it.

There are options, however, that address this problem. Much like the Brandeis story, there may be a "free bridge" option for many investors.

Your financial professional will likely tell you that it is not a matter of whether or not you should perform a Roth IRA conversion, it is a matter of how much you should convert and when.

Here are some of the things to consider before converting to a Roth IRA:

- If you make a conversion before you retire, you may end up paying higher taxes on the conversion because it is likely that you are in some of your highest earning years, placing you in the highest tax bracket of your life. It is possible that a better strategy would be to wait until after you retire, a time when you may have less taxable income, which would place you in a lower tax bracket.
- Many people opt to reduce their work hours from fulltime to part-time in the years before they retire. If you have pursued this option, your income will likely be lower, in turn lowering your tax rate.
- The first years that you draw Social Security benefits can also be years of lower reported income, making it another good time frame in which to convert to a Roth IRA.

One key strategy to handling a Roth IRA conversion is to ***always be able to pay the cost of the tax conversion with outside money***. Structuring your tax year to include something like a significant deduction can help you offset the conversion tax. This way you aren't forced to take the money you need for taxes from the value of the IRA. The reason taxes apply to this maneuver is because when you withdraw money from a traditional IRA, it is treated as taxable income by the IRS. Your financial professional, with the help of the CPAs at their firm, may be able to provide you with options like after-tax money, itemized deductions or other situations that can pose effective tax avoidance options.

Some examples of avoiding Roth IRA conversions taxes include:

- *Using medical expenses that are above 10 percent of your Adjusted Gross Income.* If you have health care costs that you can list as itemized deductions, you can convert an amount of income from a traditional IRA to a Roth IRA that is offset by the deductible amount. Essentially, deductible medical expenses negate the taxes resulting from recording the conversion.
- *Individuals, usually small business owners, who are dealing with a Net Operating Loss (NOL).* If you have NOLs, but aren't able to utilize all of them on your tax return, you can carry them forward to offset the taxable income from the taxes on income you convert to a Roth IRA.
- *Charitable giving.* If you are charitably inclined, you can use the amount of your donations to reduce the amount of taxable income you have during that year. By matching the amount you convert to a Roth IRA to the amount your taxable income was reduced by charitable giving, you can essentially avoid taxation on the conversion. You may decide to double your donations to a charity in one year, giving them two years' worth of donations in order to offset the Roth IRA conversion tax on this year's tax return.
- *Investments that are subject to depletion.* Certain investments can kick off depletion expenses. If you make an

investment and are subject to depletion expenses, they can be deducted and used to offset a Roth IRA conversion tax.

Not all of the above scenarios work for everyone, and there are many other options for offsetting conversion taxes. The point is that you have options, and your financial professional and tax professional can help you understand those options.

If you have a traditional IRA, Roth conversions are something you should look at. As you approach retirement you should consider your options and make choices that keep more of your money in your pocket, not the government's.

ADDITIONAL TAX BENEFITS OF ROTH IRAS

Not only do Roth IRAs provide you with tax-advantaged growth, they also give you a tax diversified landscape that allows you to maximize your distributions. Chances are that no matter the circumstances, you will have taxed income and other assets subject to taxation. *But if you have a Roth IRA, you have the unique ability to manage your Adjusted Gross Income (AGI), because you have a tax-advantaged income option!*

Converting to a Roth IRA can also help you preserve and build your legacy. Because Roth IRAs are exempt from RMDs, after you make a conversion from a traditional IRA, your Roth account can grow tax-advantaged for another 15, 20 or 25 years and it can be used as tax-advantaged income by your heirs. It is important to note, however, that non-spousal beneficiaries do have to take RMDs from a Roth IRA, or choose to stretch it and draw tax-advantaged income out of it over their lifetime.

TO CONVERT OR NOT TO CONVERT?

Conversions aren't only for retirees. You can convert at any time. Your choice should be based on your individual circumstances and tax situation. Sticking with a traditional IRA or converting to a Roth, again, depends on your individual circumstances, including your income, your tax bracket and the amount of deductions you have each year.

Is it better to have a Roth IRA or traditional IRA? It depends on your individual circumstance. Some people don't mind having taxable income from an IRA. Their income might not be very high and their RMD might not bump their tax bracket up, so it's not as big a deal. A similar situation might involve income from Social Security. Social Security benefits are taxed based on other income you are drawing. If you are in a position where none or very little of your Social Security benefit is subject to taxes, paying income tax on your RMD may be very easy.

There are also situations where leveraging taxable income from a traditional IRA can work to your advantage come tax time. Consider the following example:

> » *Mark and Clare dream of buying a boat when they retire. It is something they have looked forward to their entire marriage. In addition to the savings and investments that they created to supply them with income during retirement, which includes a traditional IRA, they have also saved money for the sole purpose of purchasing a boat once they stop working.*
>
> *When the time comes and they finally buy the boat of their dreams, they pay an additional $15,000 in sales taxes that year because of the large purchase. Because they are retired and earning less money, the deductions they used to be able to realize from their income taxes are no longer there. The high amount of sales taxes they paid on the boat puts them in a position where they could benefit from taking taxable income from a traditional IRA.*
>
> *When Mark and Clare's financial professional learns about their purchase, he immediately contacts a CPA at his firm to run the numbers. They determine that by taking a*

$15,000 distribution from their IRA, they could fulfill their income needs to offset the $15,000 sales tax deduction that they were claiming due to the purchase of their boat. In the end, they pay zero taxes on their income distribution from their IRA.

The moral of the story? **Having a tax diversified landscape gives you options.** Having capital assets that can be liquidated, tax-advantaged income options and sources that can create capital gains or capital losses will put you in a position to play your cards right no matter what you want to accomplish with your taxes. The ace up your sleeve is your financial professional and the CPAs they work with. Do yourself a favor and *plan* your taxes instead of *reporting* them!

CHAPTER 12 RECAP //
- Look for the "free bridge" option in your tax strategy.
- Converting from a traditional to a Roth IRA can provide you with tax-advantaged retirement income.
- Converting to a Roth IRA can also help you preserve and build your legacy.
- There are many ways to reduce your taxes. Being smart about your Roth IRA conversion is one of the main ways to do so.

13

YOUR LEGACY BEYOND DOLLARS AND CENTS

If you're like most people, planning your estate isn't on the top of your list of things to do. Planning your income needs for retirement, managing your assets and just living your life without worrying about how your estate will be handled when you are gone make legacy planning less than attractive for a Saturday afternoon task. The fact of the matter, however, is that if you don't plan your legacy, someone else will. That someone else is usually a combination of the IRS and other government entities: lawyers, executors, courts, and accountants. Who do you think has the best interests of your beneficiaries in mind?

Today, there is more consideration given to planning a legacy than just maximizing your estate. When most people think about an estate, it may seem like something only the very wealthy have: a stately manor or an enormous business. But a legacy is something else entirely. A legacy is more than the sum total of the financial assets you have accumulated. It is the lasting impression you make on those you leave behind. The dollar and cents are just a small part of a legacy.

A legacy encompasses the stories that others tell about you, shared experiences and values. An estate may pay for college tuition, but a legacy may inform your grandchildren about the importance of higher education and self-reliance.

A legacy may also contain family heirlooms or items of emotional significance. It may be a piece of art your great-grandmother painted, family photos, or a childhood keepsake.

When you go about planning your legacy, certainly explore strategies that can maximize the financial benefit to the ones you care about. But also take the time to ensure that you have organized the whole of your legacy, and let that be a part of the last gift you leave.

Many people avoid planning their legacy until they feel they must. Something may change in your life, like the birth of a grandchild, the diagnosis of a serious health problem, or the death of a close friend or loved one. Waiting for tragedy to strike in order to get your affairs in order is not the best course of action. The emotional stress of that kind of situation can make it hard to make patient, thoughtful decisions. Taking the time to create a premeditated and thoughtful legacy plan will assure that your assets will be transferred where and when you want them when the time comes.

THE BENEFITS OF PLANNING YOUR LEGACY

The distribution of your assets, whether in the form of property, stocks, Individual Retirement Accounts, 401(k)s or liquid assets, can be a complicated undertaking if you haven't left clear instructions about how you want them handled. Not having a plan will cost more money and take more time, leaving your loved ones to wait (sometimes for years) and receive less of your legacy than if you had a clear plan.

Planning your legacy will help your assets be transferred with little delay and little confusion. Instead of leaving decisions about how to distribute your estate to your family, attorneys or financial professionals, preserve your legacy and your wishes by drafting a clear plan at an early age.

And while you know all that, it can still be hard to sit down and do it. It reminds you that life is short, and the relatively complicated nature of sorting through your assets can feel like a daunting task. But one thing is for sure: *it is impossible for your assets to be transferred or distributed the way you want at the end of your life if you don't have a plan.*

One area of particular importance has to do with beneficiary designations. Many people start their careers before they start their family, so the names of current spouses and children aren't always current on these contractual agreements. Most people don't realize that even if you have a will or estate plan, it's these contractual agreements that determine who gets the money. **Beneficiary forms take precedent over last will and testament, trusts, and divorce decrees.**

This is probably the number one error we see made with legacy planning today. For federal employees, it can get even more complicated because although their survivors are entitled to benefits, they have to be done through proper beneficiary designations. Make sure your designations are up to date on the following contractual agreements:

- Life insurance
- Pension benefits
- Qualified plan money in defined-contribution plans such as TSP and 401(k) plans.
- Contributions made to defined-benefit pension plans.

When these forms aren't updated, it's the people you love who are the ones who lose out. Even with a will or trust in place, these cases often go all the way to the federal courts. Ask to have your financial professional review all your contracts to make sure that your beneficiary designations are aligned with your goals.

Ask yourself:
- Are my assets up to date?
- Have my primary and contingent beneficiaries been clearly designated?
- Does my plan allow for restriction of a beneficiary?
- Does my legacy plan address minor children that I want to provide with income?
- Does my legacy plan allow for multi-generational payout?

Answers to these questions are critical if you want the final say in how your assets are distributed. In order to achieve your legacy goals, you need a plan.

MAKING A PLAN

Eventually, when your income need is filled and you have sufficient standby money to meet your need for emergencies, travel or other extra expenses you are planning for, whatever isn't used during your lifetime becomes your financial legacy. The money that you do not use during your lifetime will either go to loved ones, unloved ones, charity, or the IRS. The question is, who would you rather disinherit?

By having a legacy plan that clearly outlines your assets, your beneficiaries and your distribution goals, you can make sure that your money and property is ending up in the hands of the people you determine beforehand. Is it really that big of a deal? It absolutely is. Think about it. Without a clear plan, it is impossible for anyone to know if your beneficiary designations are current and reflect your wishes because you haven't clearly expressed who your beneficiaries are. You may have an idea of who you want your assets to go to, but without a plan, it is anyone's guess. It is also impossible to know if the titling of your assets is accurate unless you have gone through and determined whose name is on the titles. More importantly, *if you have not clearly and effectively communicated your desires regarding the planned distribution of your legacy, you and your family may end up losing a large part of it.*

As you can see, managing a legacy is more complicated than having an attorney read your will, divide your estate and write checks to your heirs. The additional issue of taxes, Family Maximum Benefit calculations and a host of other decisions rear their heads. Educating yourself about the best options for positioning your legacy assets is a challenging undertaking. Working with a financial professional who is versed in determining the most efficient and effective ways of preserving and distributing your legacy can save you time, money and strife.

So, how do you begin?

Making a Legacy Plan Starts with a Simple List. The first, and one of the largest, steps to setting up an estate plan with a financial professional that reflects your desires is creating a detailed inventory of your assets and debts (if you have any). You need to know what assets you have, who the beneficiaries are, how much they are worth and how they are titled. You can start by identifying and listing your assets. This is a good starting point for working with a financial professional who can then help you determine the detailed information about your assets that will dictate how they are distributed upon your death.

If you are particularly concerned about leaving your kids and grandkids a lifetime of income with minimal taxes, you will want to discuss a Stretch IRA option with your financial professional.

STRETCH IRAS: GETTING THE MOST OUT OF YOUR MONEY

In 1986, the U.S. Congress passed a law that allows for multi-gen-erational distributions of IRA assets. This type of distribution is called a Stretch IRA because it stretches the distribution of the account out over a longer period of time to several beneficiaries. It also allows the account to continue accumulating value throughout your relatives' lifetimes. You can use a Stretch IRA as an income tool that distributes throughout your lifetime, your children's lifetimes and your grandchildren's lifetimes.

Stretch IRAs are an attractive option for those more concerned with creating income for their loved ones than leaving them with a lump sum that may be subject to a high tax rate. With traditional IRA distributions, non-spousal beneficiaries must generally take distributions from their inherited IRAs, whether transferred or not, within five years after the death of the IRA owner. An exception to this rule applies if the beneficiary elects to take distributions over his or her lifetime, which is referred to as stretching the IRA.

Let's begin by looking at the potential of stretching an IRA throughout multiple generations.

As the illustrations with the Cleaver family show, stretching an IRA over multiple generations can have a large impact on the total amount of income that it is able to provide. In the top illustration, Mr. Cleaver's IRA is stretched so it provides his children with multiple distributions throughout their lifetimes. By the time the account is empty, Mr. Cleaver's $350,000 IRA has been turned into a legacy of more than $1.2 million for the entire Cleaver family. But look at what happens when the IRA is not stretched: after Mr. and Mrs. Cleaver pass away, the IRA is divided between the five children and distributed to each as a single lump sum. In that scenario, the IRA only provides the Cleaver family with

Beneficiaries Stretch IRA Distributions

Mr. Cleaver's IRA Value at 64: $350,000	Mr. Cleaver's income from age 70-85: $383,251	Mr. Cleaver passes away at 85
Mrs. Cleaver passes away at 88	Mrs. Cleaver's income from age 83-88: $180,048	Mrs. Cleaver's IRA Value: $453,165

| Wally receives income of: $133,971* | Beaver receives income of: $144,008* | Eddie receives income of: $293,717* | Lumpy receives income of: $313,799* | Gilbert receives income of: $345,752* |

TOTAL INCOME TO ALL - IRA STRETCH CONCEPT: $1,231,248
Scenario assumes a 28 percent tax rate with annual rate of return of 5 percent
*Income based on RMDs of beneficiaries

Beneficiaries FAIL to Stretch IRA Distributions

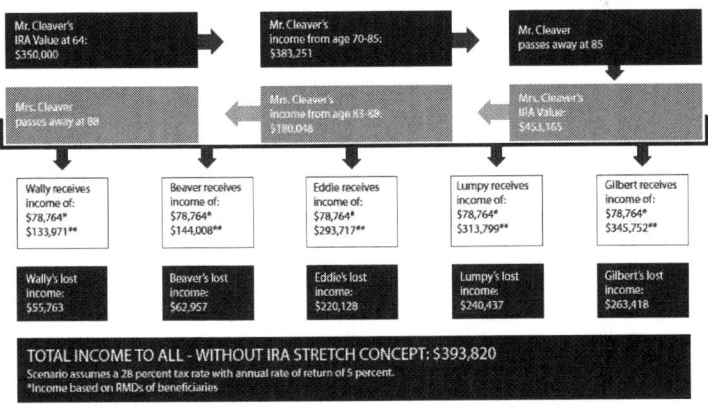

Mr. Cleaver's IRA Value at 64: $350,000	Mr. Cleaver's income from age 70-85: $383,251	Mr. Cleaver passes away at 85
Mrs. Cleaver passes away at 88	Mrs. Cleaver's income from age 83-88: $180,048	Mrs. Cleaver's IRA Value: $453,165

| Wally receives income of: $78,764* $133,971** | Beaver receives income of: $78,764* $144,008** | Eddie receives income of: $78,764* $293,717** | Lumpy receives income of: $78,764* $313,799** | Gilbert receives income of: $78,764* $345,752** |
| Wally's lost income: $55,763 | Beaver's lost income: $62,957 | Eddie's lost income: $220,128 | Lumpy's lost income: $240,437 | Gilbert's lost income: $263,418 |

TOTAL INCOME TO ALL - WITHOUT IRA STRETCH CONCEPT: $393,820
Scenario assumes a 28 percent tax rate with annual rate of return of 5 percent.
*Income based on RMDs of beneficiaries

* Lump sum after tax income upon death of Mrs. Cleaver.   ** Lifetime income based on RMD of beneficiary - see above.

a total income of $393,820. For the Cleavers, not choosing to stretch the IRA would cost them nearly $800,000 in lost income.

Unfortunately, many things may also play a role in failing to stretch IRA distributions. It can be tempting for a beneficiary to take a lump sum of money despite the tax consequences. Fortunately, if you want to solidify your plan for distribution, there are options that will allow you to open up an IRA and incorporate "spendthrift" clauses for your beneficiaries. This will ensure your legacy is stretched appropriately and to your specifications. Only certain insurance companies allow this option, and you will not find this benefit with any brokerage accounts. You need to work with a financial professional who has the appropriate relationship with an insurance company that provides this option.

CHAPTER 13 RECAP //

- Legacy planning begins with a simple list. If you don't take the time to plan your legacy, someone else will, such as the IRS, government entities, or the courts.
- The named beneficiaries on contracts such as your 401(k), life insurance policies and IRAs trump the named beneficiaries listed in a will.
- Setting up a Stretch or multi-generational IRA can ensure that your assets are distributed in a way that doesn't saddle your heirs with an excessive tax burden. It can also maximize your assets, allowing your money to grow and provide an income to your heirs for years to come.
- To avoid common IRA pitfalls, make sure to have a tax expert review your beneficiary designations with an eye for any red flags that might heap an undue tax burden on your loved ones.
- Simple legacy mistakes such as unintentional disinheritance can easily be prevented by simply taking the time to properly update your paperwork. Understand if your assets will be distributed *per stirpes* or *per capita* and make changes accordingly.

14

HOW TO AVOID THE BIG LEGACY MISTAKES

Stuart organized his assets long ago. He started planning his retirement early and made investment decisions that would meet his needs. With a combination of IRA to Roth IRA conversions, a series of income annuities and a well-planned money management strategy overseen by his financial professional, he easily filled his income gap and was able to focus on ways to accumulate his wealth throughout his retirement. He reorganized his Know So and Hope So Money as he got older. When Stuart retired, he had an income plan created that allowed him to maximize his Social Security benefit. He even had enough to accumulate wealth during his retirement. At this point, Stuart turned his attention to planning his legacy. He wanted to know how he could maximize the amount of his legacy he will pass on to his heirs.

Stuart met with an attorney to draw up a will, but he quickly learned that while having a will was a good plan, it wasn't the most efficient way to distribute his legacy. In fact, relying solely on a will created several roadblocks.

The two main problems that arose for Stuart were *Probate* and *Unintentional Disinheritance:*

Problem #1: Probate
Probate. Just speaking the word out loud can cause shivers to run down your spine. Probate's ugly reputation is well deserved. It can be a costly, time consuming process that diminishes your estate and can delay the distribution of your estate to your loved ones. Nasty stuff, by any measure. Unless you have made a clear legacy plan and discussed options for avoiding probate, it is highly likely that you have many assets that might pass through probate needlessly. ***If your will and beneficiary designations aren't correctly structured, some of these assets will go through the probate process, which can turn dollars into cents.***

If you have a will, probate is usually just a formality. There is little risk that your will won't be executed per your instructions. The problem arises when the costs and lengthy timeline that probate creates come into play. Probate proceedings are notoriously expensive, lengthy and ponderous. A typical probate process identifies all of your assets and debts, pays any taxes and fees that you owe (including estate tax), pays court fees, and distributes your property and assets to your inheritors. This process usually takes at least a year, and can take even longer before your inheritors actually receive anything that you have left for them. For this reason, and because of the sometimes exorbitant fees that may be charged by lawyers and accountants during the process, probate has earned a nasty reputation.

Probate can also be a painstakingly public process. Because the probate process happens in court, the assets you own that go through a probate procedure become part of the public record. While this may not seem like a big deal to some, other people don't want that kind of intimate information available to the public.

Additionally, if your estate is entirely distributed via your will, the money that your family may need to cover the costs of your medical bills, funeral expenses and estate taxes will be tied up in probate, which can last up to a year or more. While immediate family members may have the option of requesting immediate cash from your assets during probate to cover immediate health care expenses, taxes, and fees, that process comes with its own set of complications. Choosing alternative methods for distributing your legacy can make life easier for your loved ones and can help them claim more of your estate in a more timely fashion than traditional methods.

A simpler and less tedious approach is to avoid probate altogether by structuring your estate to be distributed outside of the probate process. Two common ways of doing this are by structuring your assets inside a life insurance plan, and by using individual retirement planning tools like IRAs that give you the option of designating a beneficiary upon your death.

Problem #2: Unintentionally Disinheriting Your Family
You would never want to unintentionally disinherit a loved one or loved ones because of confusion surrounding your legacy plan. Unfortunately, it happens. Why? This terrible situation is typically caused by a simple lack of understanding. In particular, mistakes regarding legacy distribution occur with regards to those whom people care for the most: their grandchildren.

One of the most important ways to plan for the inheritance of your grandchildren is by properly structuring the distribution of your legacy. Specifically, you need to know if your legacy is going to be distributed *per stirpes* or *per capita*.

Per Stirpes. *Per stirpes* is a legal term in Latin that means "by the branch." Your estate will be distributed *per stirpes* if you designate each branch of your family to receive an equal share of your estate. In the event that your children predecease you, their share will be distributed evenly between their children—your grandchildren.

Per Capita. *Per capita* distribution is different in that you may designate different amounts of your estate to be distributed to members of the same generation.

Per stirpes distribution of assets will follow the family tree down the line as the predecessor beneficiaries pass away. On the other hand, per capita distribution of assets ends on the branch of the family tree with the death of a designated beneficiary. For example, when your child passes away, in a per capita distribution, your grandchildren would not receive distributions from the assets that you designated to your child.

What the terms mean is not nearly as important as what they do, however. The reality is that improperly titled assets could accidentally leave your grandchildren disinherited upon the death of their parents. It's easy to check, and it's even easier to fix.

A simple way to remember the difference between the two types of distribution goes something like this: "*Stirpes are forever and Capita is capped.*"

Another way to avoid complicated legacy distribution problems, and the probate process, is by leveraging a life insurance plan.

LIFE INSURANCE: AN IMPORTANT LEGACY TOOL

One of the most powerful legacy tools you can leverage is a good life insurance policy. Life insurance is a highly efficient legacy tool because it creates money when it is needed or desired the most. Over the years, life insurance has become less expensive, while it offers more features, and it provides longer guarantees.

There are many unique benefits of life insurance that can help your beneficiaries get the most out of your legacy. Some of them include:
- Providing beneficiaries with a tax-free, liquid asset.
- Covering the costs associated with your death.
- Providing income for your dependents.
- Offering an investment opportunity for your beneficiaries.
- Covering expenses such as tuition or mortgage down payments for your children or grandchildren.

Very few people want life insurance, but nearly everyone wants what it does. Life insurance is specifically, and uniquely, capable of creating money when it is needed most. When a loved one passes, no amount of money can remove the pain of loss. And certainly, money doesn't solve the challenges that might arise with losing someone important.

It has been said that when you have money, you have options. When you don't have money, your options are severely limited. You might imagine a life insurance policy can give your family and loved ones options that would otherwise be impossible.

> » *Ethan spent the last 20 years building a small business. In so many ways, it is a family business. Each of his three children, Maddie, Ruby and Owen, worked in the shop part-time during high school. But after all three attended college, only Maddie returned to join her father, and eventually will run the business full-time when Ethan retires.*
>
> *Ethan is able to retire comfortably on Social Security and on-going income from the shop, but the business is nearly his entire financial legacy. It is his wish that Maddie own the business outright, but he also wants to leave an equal legacy to each of his three children.*

> *There is no simple way to divide the business into thirds and still leave the business intact for Maddie.*
>
> *Ethan ends up buying a life insurance policy to make up the difference. Ruby and Owen will receive their share of an inheritance in cash from the life insurance policy and Maddie will be able to inherit the business intact.*
>
> *Ethan is able to accomplish his goals, treat all three children equitably and leave Maddie the business she helped to build.*

If you have a life insurance policy but you haven't looked at it in a while, you may not know how it operates, how much it is worth and how it will be distributed to your beneficiaries. You may also need to update your beneficiaries on your policy. In short, without a comprehensive review of your policy, you don't really know where the money will go or to whom it will go.

If you don't have a life insurance policy but are looking for options to maintain and grow your legacy, speaking with a professional can show you the benefits of life insurance. Many people don't consider buying a life insurance policy until some event in their life triggers it, like the loss of a loved one, an accident or a health condition.

BENEFITS OF LIFE INSURANCE

Life insurance is a useful and secure tool for contingency planning, ensuring that your dependents receive the assets that you want them to have, and for meeting the financial goals you have set for the future. While it bears the name "Life Insurance," it is, in reality, a diverse financial tool that can meet many needs. The main function of a life insurance policy is to provide financial assets for your survivors. Life insurance is particularly efficient at achieving this goal because it provides a tax-advantaged lump sum of money in the form of a death benefit to your beneficiary or beneficiaries. That financial asset can be used in a number of ways. It can be structured as an investment to provide income for your spouse or children, it can pay down debts, and it can be used to cover estate taxes and other costs associated with death.

Tax liabilities on the estate you leave behind are inevitable. Capital property, for instance, is taxed at its fair market value at the time of your death, unless that property is transferred to your spouse. If the property has appreciated during the time you owned it, taxation on capital gains will occur. Registered Retirement Savings Plans (RRSPs) and other similarly structured assets are also included as taxable income unless transferred to a beneficiary as well. Those are just a few examples of how an estate can become subject to a heavy tax burden. The unique benefits of a life insurance policy provide ways to handle this tax burden, solving any liquidity problems that may arise if your family members want to hold onto an illiquid asset, such as a piece of property or an investment. Life insurance can provide a significant amount of money to a family member or other beneficiary, and that money is likely to remain exempt from taxation or seizure.

One of life insurance's most important benefits is that it is not considered part of the estate of the policy holder. The death benefit that is paid by the insurance company goes exclusively to the beneficiaries listed on the policy. This shields the proceeds of the policy from fees and costs that can reduce an estate, including probate proceedings, attorneys' fees and claims made by creditors. The distribution of your life insurance policy is also unaffected by delays of the estate's distribution, like probate. Your beneficiaries will get the proceeds of the policy in a timely fashion, regardless of how long it takes for the rest of your estate to be settled.

Investing a portion of your assets in a life insurance policy can also protect that portion of your estate from creditors. If you owe money to someone or some entity at the time of your death, a creditor is not able to claim any money from a life insurance policy or an annuity, for that matter. An exception to this rule is if you had already used the life insurance policy as collateral against a loan. If a large portion of the money you want to dedicate to your legacy is sitting in a savings account, investment or other liquid form, creditors may be able to receive their claim on it before your beneficiaries get anything, that is if there's anything left. A life insurance policy protects your assets from creditors and ensures that your beneficiaries get the money that you intend them to have.

HOW MUCH LIFE INSURANCE DO YOU NEED?

Determining the type of policy and the amount right for you depends on an analysis of your needs. A financial professional can help you complete a needs analysis that will highlight the amount of insurance that you require to meet your goals. This type of personalized review will allow you to determine ways to continue providing income for your spouse or any dependents you may have. A financial professional can also help you calculate the amount of income that your policy should replace to meet the needs of your beneficiaries and the duration of the distribution of that income.

You may also want to use your life insurance policy to meet any expenses associated with your death. These can include funeral costs, fees from probate and legal proceedings, and taxes. You may also want to dedicate a portion of your policy proceeds to help fund tuition or other expenses for your children or grandchildren. You can buy a policy and hope it covers all of those costs, or you can work with a professional who can calculate exactly how much insurance you need and how to structure it to meet your goals. Which would you rather do?

AVOIDING POTENTIAL SNAGS

There are benefits to having life insurance supersede the direction given in a will or other estate plan, but there are also some potential snags that you should address to meet your wishes. For example, if your will instructs that your assets be divided equally between your two children but your life insurance beneficiary is listed as just one of the children, the assets in the life insurance policy will only be distributed to the child listed as the beneficiary. The beneficiary designation of your life insurance supersedes your will's instruction. This is important to understand when designating beneficiaries on a policy you purchase. Work with a professional to make sure that your beneficiaries are accurately listed on your assets, especially your life insurance policies.

USING LIFE INSURANCE TO BUILD YOUR LEGACY

Depending on your goals, there are strategies you can use that could multiply how much you leave behind. Life insurance is one of the most surefire and efficient investment tools for building a substantial legacy that will meet your financial goals.

Here is a brief overview of how life insurance can boost your legacy:

- Life insurance provides an immediate increase in your legacy.
- It provides an income tax-advantaged death benefit for your beneficiaries.
- A good life insurance policy has the opportunity to accumulate value over time.
- It may have an option to include long-term care (LTC) or chronic illness benefits should you require them.

If your Green Money income needs for retirement are met and you have Managed Money assets that will provide for your future expenses, you may have extra assets that you want to earmark as legacy funds. By electing to invest those assets into a life insurance policy, you can immediately increase the amount of your legacy. Remember, **life insurance allows you to transfer a tax-advantaged lump sum of money to your beneficiaries. It remains in your control during your lifetime, can provide for your long-term care needs and bypasses probate costs.** And make no mistake, taxes can have a huge impact on your legacy. Not only that, income and assets from your legacy can have tax implications for your beneficiaries, as well.

Here's a brief overview of how taxes could affect your legacy and your beneficiaries:

- The higher your income, the higher the rate at which it is taxed.
- Withdrawals from qualified plans are taxed as income.
- What's more, when you leave a large qualified plan, it ends up being taxed at a high rate.
- If you left a $500,000 IRA to your child, they could end up owing as much as $140,000 in income taxes.
- However, if you could just withdraw $50,000 a year, the tax bill might only be $10,000 per year.

How could you use that annual amount to leave a larger legacy? Luckily, you can leverage a life insurance policy to avoid those tax penalties, preserving a larger amount of your legacy and freeing your beneficiaries from an added tax burden.

> » *When Gabby turned 70 years old, she decided it was time to look into life insurance policy options. She still feels young, but she remembers that her mother died in early 70s, and she wants to plan ahead so she can pass on some of her legacy to her grandchildren just like her grandmother did for her.*
>
> *Gabby doesn't really want to think about life insurance, but she does want the security, reliability and tax-advantaged*

distribution that it offers. She lives modestly, and her Social Security benefit meets most of her income needs. As the beneficiary of her late husband's Certificate of Deposit (CD), she has $100,000 in an account that she has never used and doesn't anticipate ever needing since her income needs were already met.

*After looking at several different investment options with a professional, Gabby decides that a Single Premium life insurance policy fits her needs best. She can buy the policy with a $100,000 one-time payment and she is guaranteed that it would provide more than the value of the contract to her beneficiaries. If she left the money in the CD, it would be subject to taxes. But for every dollar that she puts into the life insurance policy, her beneficiaries are guaranteed at least that dollar plus a death benefit, and all of it will be **tax-free**!*

For $100,000, Gabby's particular policy offers a $170,000 death benefit distribution to her beneficiaries. By moving the $100,000 from a CD to a life insurance policy, Gabby increases her legacy by 70 percent. Not only that, she has also sheltered it from taxes, so her beneficiaries will be able to receive $1.70 for every $1.00 that she entered into the policy! While buying the policy doesn't allow her to use the money for herself, it does allow her family to benefit from her well-planned legacy.

MAKE YOUR WISHES KNOWN

Estate taxes used to be a much hotter topic in the mid-2000s when the estate tax limits and exclusions were much smaller and taxed at a higher rate than today. In 2008, estates valued at $2 million or more were taxed at 45 percent. Just two years later, the limit was raised to $5 million dollars taxed at 35 percent. The limit has continued to rise ever since. The limit applies to fewer people than before. Estate organization, however, is just as important as ever, and it affects everyone.

Ask yourself:
- Are your assets actually titled and held the way you think they are?
- Are your beneficiaries set up the way you think they should be?
- Have there been changes to your family or those you desire as beneficiaries?

There is more to your legacy beyond your property, money, investments and other assets that you leave to family members, loved ones and charities. Everyone has a legacy beyond money. You also leave behind personal items of importance, your values and beliefs, your personal and family history, and your wishes. Beyond a will and a plan for your assets, it is important that you make your wishes known to someone for the rest of your personal legacy. When it comes time for your family and loved ones to make decisions after you are gone, knowing your wishes can help them make decisions that honor you and your legacy, and give meaning to what you leave behind. Your professional can help you organize.

Think about your:
- Personal stories / recollections
- Values
- Personal items of emotional significance
- Financial assets

Do you want to make a plan to pass these things on to your family?

WORKING WITH A PROFESSIONAL

Part of using life insurance to your greatest advantage is selecting the policy and provider that can best meet your goals. Venturing into the jungle of policies, brokers and salespeople can be overwhelming, and can leave you wondering if you've made the best decision. Working with a trusted financial professional can help you cut through the red tape, the "sales-speak" and confusion to find a policy that meets your goals and best serves your desires for your money. If you already have a policy, a financial professional can help you review it and become familiar with the policy's premium, the guarantees the policy affords, its performance, and its features and benefits. A financial professional can also help you make any necessary changes to the policy.

> » *When Kristi turned 88, her daughter finally convinced her to meet with a financial professional to help her organize her assets and get her legacy in order. Although Kristi is reluctant to let a stranger in on her personal finances, she ends up very glad that she did.*
>
> *In the process of listing Kristi's assets and her beneficiaries, her professional finds a man's name listed as the beneficiary of an old life insurance annuity that she owns. It turns out, the man is Kristi's ex-husband who is still alive. Had Kristi passed away before her ex-husband, the annuities and any death benefits that came with them, would have been passed on to her ex-husband. This does not reflect her latest wishes.*

Things change, relationships evolve and the way you would like your legacy organized needs to adapt to the changes that happen throughout your life. There may be a new child or grandchild in your family, or you may have been divorced or remarried. A professional will regularly review your legacy assets and ask you questions to make sure that everything is up to date and that the current organization reflects your current wishes.

CHAPTER 14 RECAP //
- Organizing your estate will ensure your wishes are properly carried through so you can effectively control your estate from the grave. Working with a financial professional can help avoid the ponderous and expensive probate process. Your professional can also make sure that you aren't unintentionally disinheriting your heirs.
- To avoid unintentional disinheritance, understand the difference between the designations *per stirpes* and *per capita*.
- Life insurance provides for the distribution of tax-free, liquid assets to your beneficiaries and can significantly build your legacy. They can also provide Living Benefits to help you pay for the high costs of medical care while you are still living.
- Working with a financial professional can help you select the policy that best meets your needs, or can help you fine tune your existing policy to better reflect your desires and intentions.

15
CHOOSING A QUALIFIED RETIREMENT PRO

From the moment you dip your toes into the retirement planning pool to the point you start swimming laps, your assets organized, your income needs met, and your accumulation and legacy plans in place, working with a professional that you trust can make all the difference in how well your retirement reflects your desires.

It is important to know what you are looking for before taking the plunge. There are many people that would love to handle your money, but not everyone is qualified to handle it in a way that leads to a holistic approach to creating a solid retirement plan.

The distinction being made here is that you should look for someone that puts your interests first and actively wants to help you meet your goals and objectives. Oftentimes, the products someone sells you matter less than their dedication to making sure that you have a plan that meets your needs.

Professionals take your whole financial position into consideration. They make plans that adjust your risk exposure, invest in tools that secure your desired income during retirement and create investment strategies that allow you to continue accumulating wealth during your retirement for you to use later or to contribute to your legacy. If you buy stocks with a broker, use a different agent for a life insurance policy and have an unmanaged 401(k) through your employer, working with a financial professional will consolidate the management of your assets so you have one trustworthy person quarterbacking all of the team elements of your portfolio. Financial products and investment tools change, but the concepts that lie behind wise retirement planning are lasting. In the end, a financial professional's approach is designed for those serious about planning for retirement. *Can you say the same thing about the person that advises you about your financial life?*

It's easy to see how choosing a financial professional can be one of the most important decisions you can make in your life. Not only do they provide you with advice, they also manage the personal assets that supply your retirement income and contribute to your legacy. So, how do you find a good one?

HOW TO FIND A FINANCIAL PROFESSIONAL YOU CAN TRUST

Taking care to select a financial professional is one of the best things you can do for yourself and for your future. Your professional has influence and control of your investment decisions, making their role in your life more than just important. Your financial security and the quality of your retirement depends on the decisions, investment strategies and asset structuring that you and your professional create.

CHOOSING A QUALIFIED RETIREMENT PRO

Working with a professional is different than calling up a broker when you want to buy or trade some stock. This isn't a decision that you can hand off to anyone else. You need to bring your time and attention to the table when it comes to finding someone with whom you can entrust your financial life. Separating the wheat from the chaff will take some work, but you'll be happy you did it.

While no one can tell you exactly who to choose or how to choose them, the following information can help you narrow the field:

- You can start by asking your friends, family and colleagues for referrals. You will want to pay particular attention to the recommendations that you get from others who are in your similar financial situation and who have similar lifestyle choices. The professional for the CEO of your company may have a different skill-set than the skill-set of the professional befitting your cousin who has 3 kids and a Subaru like you. Do follow-up research on the Internet as well. Look up the people who have been recommended to you on websites like LinkedIn that show the work history, referrals and experience of the candidates that you find most attractive. You will also learn about the firms with or for whom they work. The investment philosophies and reputations of the companies they work for will tell you a lot about how they will handle your money.

- The other side of the coin, however, is that everyone and their brother has a recommendation about how you should manage your money and who should manage it for you. From hot stock tips to "the best money manager in the state," people love to share good information that makes them look like they are in-the-know. Nobody wants to talk about the bad stock purchases they made, the times they lost money and the poor selections they made regarding financial professionals or stock brokers.

If you decide to take a friend or family member's recommendation, make sure they have a substantial, long-term experience with the financial professional and that their glowing review isn't just based on a one-time "win."
- It is important to understand how your professional is being paid. It is generally considered preferable to work with a fee-based professional who will not have conflicts of interests between earning a commission and acting in your best interests.
- Many professionals may also be brokers or dealers that can earn commissions on things like life insurance, certain types of annuities and disability insurance. These professionals have most likely intentionally overlapped their roles so that if their clients choose to purchase insurance or investment products that require a broker or dealer, those clients won't have to find an additional person to work with. Again, understanding the role of your professional will help you make your determination.

NARROWING THE FIELD

1. Decide on the Type of Professional with Whom You Want to Work. There are four basic kinds of financial professionals. Many professionals may play overlapping roles. It is important to know a professional's primary function, how they charge for their services and whether they are obligated to act in your best interest.

Registered representatives, better known as stockbrokers or bank / investment representatives, make their living by earning commissions on insurance products and investment services. Stockbrokers basically sell you things. The products from which they make the highest commission are sometimes the products that they recommend to their clients. If you want to make a simple transaction, such as buying or selling a particular stock, a registered representative can help you. Although registered representatives are licensed professionals, if you want to create a structured and planful approach to positioning your assets for retirement, you might want to consider continuing your search.

The term "planner" is often misused. It can refer to credible professionals that are CPAs, CFPs and ChFCs to your uncle's next door neighbor who claims to have a lead on some undervalued stock about to be "discovered." A wide array of people may claim to be planners because there are no requirements to be a planner. The term financial planner, however, refers to someone who is properly registered as an investment advisor and serves as a fiduciary as described below.

Financial professionals are the diamonds in the rough. These Registered Investment Advisors are compensated on a fee basis. They do, however, often have licensure as stockbrokers or insurance agents, allowing them to earn commissions on certain transactions. More importantly, **financial professionals are financial fiduciaries, meaning they are required to make financial decisions in your best interest and reflecting your risk tolerance.** Investment Advisors are held to high ethical standards and are highly regarded in the financial industry. Financial professionals also often take a more comprehensive approach to asset management. These professionals are trained and credentialed to plan and coordinate their clients' assets in order to meet their goals or retirement and legacy planning. They are not focused on individual stocks, investments or markets. They look at the big picture, the whole enchilada.

Money managers are on par with financial professionals. However, they are often given explicit permission to make investment decisions without advanced approval by their clients.

Understanding who you are working with and what their title is the first step to planning your retirement. While each of the above-mentioned types of financial professionals can help you with aspects of your finances, it is **financial professionals** who have the most intimate role, the most objective investment strategies and the most unbiased mode of compensation for their services. A financial professional can also help you with the non-financial aspects of your legacy and can help you find ways to create a tax planning strategy to help you save money.

2. Be Objective. At the end of the day, you need to separate the weak from the strong. While you might want a strong personal rapport with your professional, or you may want to choose your professional for their personality and positive attitude, it is more important that you find someone who will give sage advice regarding achieving your retirement goals.

It can be helpful to use a process of elimination to narrow the field of potential professionals. Look into five or six potential leads and cross off your list the ones that don't meet your requirements until only one or two remain. Cross-check your remaining choices against the list of things you need from a professional. Make sure they represent a firm that has the investment tools and products that you desire, and make sure they have experience in retirement planning. That is, after all, the main goal.

Don't be afraid to investigate each of your candidates. You'll want to ask the same questions and look for the same information from everyone you consider so you can then compare them and discern which is best for you. You'll want to take a look at the specific credentials of each professional, their experience and competence, their ethics and fiduciary status, their history and track record, and a list of the services that they offer. The professionals who meet all or most of your qualifications are the ones you will contact for an interview.

Potential professionals should meet your qualifications in the following categories:
- *Credentials:* Look at their experience, the quality of their education, any associations to which they belong

and certifications they have earned. Someone who has continued their professional education through ongoing certifications will be more up-to-date on current financial practices compared to someone who got their degree 25 years ago and hasn't done a thing since.
- *Practices:* Look at the track record of your candidates, how they are compensated for their services, the reports and analysis they offer, and their value added services.
- *Services:* Your professional must meet your needs. If you are planning your retirement, you should work with someone who offers services that help you to that end. You want someone who can offer planning, advice on investment strategies, ways to calculate risk, advice on insurance and annuities products, and ways to manage your tax strategy.
- *Ethics:* You want to work with someone who is above board and does things the right way. Vet them by checking their compliance record, current licensing, fiduciary status and, yes, even their criminal record. You never know!

3. Ask for and Check References. Once you have selected two or three professionals that you want to meet, call or email them and ask for references. Every professional should be able to provide you with at least two or three names. In fact, they will probably be eager to share them with you. Most professionals rely on references for validation of their success, quality of services and likability. You should, however, take them with a grain of salt. You have no way to know whether or not references are a professional's friends or colleagues.

It is worth contacting references, however, to check for inconsistencies. Ask each reference the same set of questions to get the same basic information. How long have they been working with the professional? What kind of services have they used and were they happy with them? What type of financial planning did they use the professional for? Were they versed in the type of financial planning that you needed? You can also ask them direct questions to elicit candid responses. What was the full cost of the expenses that your professional charged you? Do the reports and statements you receive come from the same firm? Questions like these can help you get a sense of how well the reference knows their professional and whether or not they are a quality reference.

A good reference is a bit like icing on the cake. It's nice to have them, but nothing speaks louder than a good track record and quality experience. And remember that a good reference, while nice to hear, is relatively cheap. How many times have you heard someone on the golf course or at work telling you how great their stockbroker is? But how many times have you heard about the bad investments or losses they have experienced?

4. Use the Internet. As a final step before picking up the phone and calling your candidates, do some digging to discover if anyone on your list has a history of unlawful or unethical practices, or has been disciplined for any of their professional behavior or decisions. Don't worry, you don't have to hire a private investigator. You can easily find this information on the Financial Industry Regulatory Authority's (FINRA) online BrokerCheck tool: http://www.finra.org/Investors/ToolsCalculators/BrokerCheck/.

You should obviously explore the website of a potential professional and the website of the firm that they represent. The Internet allows you to go beyond the online business card of a professional to gain access to information that they don't control. It may all be good information! Or a brief search of the Internet could reveal a sketchy past. The best part is that the Internet allows you to find helpful information in an anonymous fashion.

Start with Google (www.google.com) and search the name of a potential professional and their firm. Keep your eyes trained on third party sources such as articles, blog posts or news stories that mention the professional. You can also check a professional's compliance records online with the Financial Industry Regulatory Authority (FINRA) and the Securities and Exchange Commission (SEC). If you want to dig deeper, you can combine search terms like "scams," "lawsuits," "suspensions" and "fraud" with a professional's or firm's name to see what information arises. More likely than not, you won't find anything. But if you do, you'll be glad that you checked.

HOW TO INTERVIEW CANDIDATES

After vetting your candidates and narrowing down a list of professionals that you think might be a good fit for you, it's time to start interviewing.

When you meet in person with a professional, you want to take advantage of your time with them. The presentations and information that they share with you will be important to pay attention to, but you will also want to control some aspects of the interview. After a professional has told you what they want you to hear, it's time to ask your own questions to get the specific information you need to make your decision.

Make sure to prepare a list of questions and an informal agenda so that you can keep track of what you want to ask and what points you want the professional to touch on during the interview. Using the same questions and agenda will also allow you to more easily compare the professionals after you have interviewed them all. Remember that these interviews are just that, *interviews*. You are meeting with several professionals to determine with whom you want to work. Don't agree to anything or sign anything during an interview until after you have made your final decision.

It can also be helpful to put a time limit on your interviews and to meet the professionals at their offices. The time limit will keep things on track and will allow structured time for presentations and questions/discussion. By meeting them at their office, you can get a sense of the work environment, the staff culture and attitude, and how the firm does business. If you are unable to travel to a professional's office and must meet them at your home or office, make sure that your interviews are scheduled with plenty of time between so the professionals don't cross each other's paths.

You can use the following questions during an initial interview to get an understanding of how each professional does business and whether they are a good fit for you:

1. How do you charge for your services? How much do you charge? This information should be easy to find on their website, but if you don't see it, ask. Find out if they charge an initial planning fee, if they charge a percentage for assets under their management and if they make money by selling specific financial products or services. If so, you should follow up by asking how much the service costs. This will give you an idea of how they really make their money and if they have incentive to sell certain products over others. Make sure you understand exactly how you will be charged so there are no surprises down the road if you decide to work with this person.

2. What are your credentials, licenses, and certifications? There are Certified Financial Planners (CFPs), Chartered Financial Consultants (ChFCs), Investment Advisor Representatives, Certified Public Accountants (CPAs) and Personal Financial Specialists (PFSs). Whatever their credentials or titles, you want to be sure that the professional you work with is an expert in the field relevant to your circumstances. If you want someone to manage your money, you will most likely look for an Investment Advisor. Someone that works with an independent firm will likely have a team of CPAs, CFPs and other financial experts upon whom they can draw. If you like the professional you are meeting with and you think they might be a good fit, but they don't have the accounting experience you want them to have, ask about their firm and the resources available to them. If they work closely with CPAs that are experienced in your needs, it could be a good match.

3. What are the financial services that you and your firm provide? The question within the question here is, "Can you help me achieve my goals?" Some people can only provide you with investment advice, and others are tax consultants. You will likely want to work with someone that provides a complete suite of financial planning services and products that touch on retirement planning, insurance options, legacy and estate structuring, and tax planning. Whatever services they provide, make sure they meet your needs and your anticipated needs.

4. What kinds of clients do you work with the most? A lot of financial professionals work within a niche: retirement planning, risk assessment, life insurance, etc. Finding someone who works with other people that are in the same financial boat as you and who have similar goals can be an important way to make sure they understand your needs. While someone might be a crackerjack annuities cowboy, you might not be interested in that option. Ask follow-up questions that will really help you understand where their expertise lies and whether or not their experience lines up with your needs.

5. May I see a sample of one of your financial plans? You wouldn't buy a car without test driving it, and you should not work with a professional without seeing a sample of how they do business. While there is no formal structure that a financial plan has to follow, the variation between professionals can help you find someone who "speaks your language." One professional may provide you with an in-depth analysis that relies heavily on info graphics and diagrams. Someone else may give you a seven page review of your assets and general recommendations. By seeing a sample plan, you can narrow down who presents information in the way that you desire and in ways that you understand.

6. How do you approach investing? You may be entirely in the dark about how to approach your investments, or you might have some guiding principles. Either way, ask each candidate what their philosophy is. Some will resonate with you and some won't. A good professional who has a realistic approach to investing won't promise you the moon or tell you that they can make you a lot of money. Professionals who are successful at retirement planning and full service financial management will tell you that they will listen to your goals, risk tolerance and comfort level with different types of investment strategies. Working with someone that you trust is critical, and this question in particular can help you find out who you can and who you can't.

7. How do you remain in contact with your clients? Does your prospective professional hold annual, quarterly or monthly meetings? How often do *you* want to meet with your professional? Some people want to check in once a year, go over everything and make sure their ducks are all in a row. If any changes over the previous year or additions to their legacy planning strategy came up, they'll do it on that date. Other people want a monthly update to be more involved in the decision making process and to understand what's happening with their portfolio. You basically need to determine the right degree of involvement for both you and your financial professional. You'll also want to feel out how your professional communicates. Do you prefer phone calls or face-to-face meetings? Do you want your professional to explain things to you in detail or to summarize for you what decisions they've made? Is the professional willing to give you their direct phone number or their email address? More importantly, do you want that information and do you want to be able to contact them in those ways?

8. Are you my main contact, or do you work with a team? This is another way of finding out how involved with you your professional will be, and how often they will meet with you. It is also a way to discover how the firm they represent operates and manages their clients. Some professionals will answer their own phone, meet with you regularly and have your home phone number on speed dial. Others will meet with you once a year and have a partner or assistant check in with you every quarter to give you an update. Other companies take an entirely team-based approach whereby clients have a main contact but their portfolio is handled by a team of professionals that represent the firm. One way isn't better than another, but one way will be best for you. Find out how the professional you are interviewing operates before entering into an agreement.

9. How do you provide a unique experience for your clients? This is a polite way of asking, "Why should I work with you?" A professional should have a compelling answer to this question that connects with you. Their answer will likely touch on their investment philosophy, their communication style and their expertise. If you hear them describing strengths and philosophies that resonate with you, keep them on your list. Some professionals will tell you that they will make investments with your money that match your values, others will say they will maximize your returns and others will say they will protect your capital while structuring your assets for income. Whatever you're looking for in a professional, you will most likely find it in the answer to this question.

This last question you will want to ask *yourself* after you've met with someone who you are considering hiring:

10. Did they ask questions and show signs that they were interested in working with me? A professional who will structure your assets to reflect your risk tolerance and to position you for a comfortable retirement must be a good listener. You will want to pass by a professional who talks non-stop and tells you what to do without listening to what you want them to do. If you felt they listened well and understood your needs, and seemed interested and experienced in your situation, then they might be right for you.

THE IMPORTANCE OF INDEPENDENCE

Not all investment firms and financial professionals are created equal. The information in this book has systematically shown that leveraging investments for income and accumulation in today's market requires new ideas and modern planning. In short, you need innovative ideas to come up with the creative solutions that will provide you with the retirement that you want. Innovation thrives on independence. No matter how good a financial professional is, the firm that they represent needs to operate on principles that make sense in today's economy. Remember, advice about money has been around forever. Good advice, however, changes with the times.

Timing the market, relying on the sale of stocks for income and banking on high treasury and bond returns are not strategies. They aren't even realistic ways to make money or to generate income. Working with an independent agent can help you break free from the old ways of thinking and position you to create a realistic retirement plan.

Working with an independent professional who relies on fee-based income tied to the success of their performance will also

give you greater peace of mind. When you do well, they do well, and that's the way it should be. Your independent financial professional will make sure that:
- Your assets are organized and structured to reflect your risk tolerance.
- Your assets will be available to you when you need them and in the way that you need them.
- You will have a lifetime income that will support your lifestyle through your retirement.
- You are handling your taxes as efficiently as possible.
- Your legacy is in order.
- Your Red Money is turned into Yellow Money, and is managed in your best interest.

» *Remember Dave and Lori from Chapter 1? Even though they knew they had Social Security benefits coming, they placed some money in savings and each had a pension or a 401(k). Before they met with a financial professional, they had no idea what their retirement would look like. After they met with an agent, they knew exactly what types of assets they had, how much they were worth, how much risk they were exposed to and how they were going to be distributed. They also created an income plan so that they could pay their bills every month the moment they retired, and they maximized their Social Security benefit by targeting the year and month they would get the most lifetime benefits. After their income needs were met, they were able to continue accumulating wealth by investing their extra assets to serve them in the future and contribute to their legacy. Their professional also helped them make decisions that impacted their taxes, protecting the value of their assets and allowing them to keep more of their money.*

This isn't a fairy tale scenario. This is an example of how much you stand to gain by meeting with a financial professional who can help you create a planful approach to your retirement. The concept of Know So and Hope So didn't just apply to their money, it also applied to Dave and Lori. They hoped that they would have enough for retirement and that they had worked hard enough and saved enough to maintain their lifestyle. Working with a financial professional allowed them to know that their income needs were secured and structured to provide them with income for the rest of their lives and with some money to spare.

Now, ask yourself: Is your retirement built on hopes and dreams, or a solid, predictable plan?

IT'S WORTH IT!

Finding, interviewing and selecting a financial professional can seem like a daunting task. And honestly, it will take a good amount of work to narrow the field and find the one you want. In the end, it is worth the blood, sweat and tears. Your retirement, lifestyle, assets and legacy is on the line. The choices you make today will have lasting impacts on your life and the life of your loved ones. Working with someone you trust and know you can rely on to make decisions that will benefit you is invaluable. The work it takes to find them is something you will never regret.

Here is a recap of why working with a financial professional is the best retirement decision you can make:

CHAPTER 15 RECAP //

- Look for professionals held to fiduciary standards of liability who put your interests first and actively want to help you meet your goals and objectives. Your risk tolerance, needs, liquidity concerns and timeline worries should be the focus of the meeting before they try to sell you any products.
- Ask family and friends for referrals. Make sure to do your due diligence and check out the references of anyone who is recommended to you. Look for resources online such as the Financial Planning Association and the National Association of Personal Financial professionals.
- When interviewing candidates, ask questions such as, "How often do you check in with your clients?" "May I see a sample of one of your financial plans?" and, "How do you approach investing?" These questions will help ensure that you and your professional are a good fit for each other.
- Not all investment firms and financial professionals are created equal. Working with an independent professional will give you more options that are customizable to your life.

GLOSSARY*

ANNUAL RESET *(ANNUAL RATCHET, CLIQUET)* – Crediting methods measuring index movement over a one year period. Positive interest is calculated and credited at the end of each contract year and cannot be lost if the index subsequently declines. Say that the index increased from 100 to 110 in one year and the indexed annuity had an 80 percent participation rate. The insurance company would take the 10 percent gross index gain for the year (110-100/100), apply the participation rate (10 percent index gain x 80 percent rate) and credit 8 percent interest to the annuity. But, what if in the following year the index declined back to 100? The individual would keep the 8 percent interest earned and simply receive zero interest for the down year. An annual reset structure

---

* *"Glossary of Terms." FixedAnnuityFacts.com. NAFA, the National Association for Fixed Annuities, n.d. 12 Nov. 2013*

preserves credited gains and treats negative index periods as years with zero growth.

ANNUITANT – The person, usually the annuity owner, whose life expectancy is used to calculate the income payment amount on the annuity.

ANNUITY – An annuity is a contract issued by an insurance company that often serves as a type of savings plan used by individuals looking for long term growth and protection of assets that will likely be needed within retirement.

AVERAGING – Index values may either be measured from a start point to an end point (point-to-point) or values between the start point and end point may be averaged to determine an ending value. Index values may be averaged over the days, weeks, months or quarters of the period.

BENEFICIARY – A beneficiary is the person designated to receive payments due upon the death of the annuity owner or the annuitant themselves.

BONUS RATE – A bonus rate is the "extra" or "additional" interest paid during the first year (the initial guarantee period), typically used as an added incentive to get consumers to select their annuity policy over another.

CALL OPTION *(ALSO SEE PUT OPTION)* – Gives the holder the right to buy an underlying security or index at a specified price on or before a given date.

CAP – The maximum interest rate that will be credited to the annuity for the year or period. The cap usually refers to the maximum interest credited after applying the participation rate or yield spread. If the index methodology showed a 20 percent increase, the participation rate was 60 percent and the maximum interest cap was 10 percent, the contract would credit 10 percent interest. A few annuities use a maximum gain cap instead of a maximum interest cap with the participation rate or yield spread applied to the lesser of the gain or the cap. If the index methodology showed a 20 percent increase, the participation rate was 60 percent and the maximum gain cap was 10 percent, the contract would credit 6 percent interest.

COMPOUND INTEREST – Interest is earned on both the original principal and on previously earned interest. It is more favorable than simple interest. Suppose that your original principal was $1 and your interest rate was 10 percent for five years. With simple interest, your value is ($1 + $0.10 interest each year) = $1.50. With compound interest, your value is ($1 x 1.10 x 1.10 x 1.10 x 1.10 x 1.10) = $1.61. The advantage of compound interest over simple interest becomes greater as each subsequent period passes.

CREDITING METHOD (ALSO SEE METHODOLOGY) – The formula(s) used to determine the excess interest that is credited above the minimum interest guarantee.

DEATH BENEFITS – The payment the annuity owner's estate or beneficiaries will receive if he or she dies before the annuity matures. On most annuities, this is equal to the current account value. Some annuities offer an enhanced value at death via an optional rider that has a monthly or annual fee associated with it.

EXCESS INTEREST – Interest credited to the annuity contract above the minimum guaranteed interest rate. In an indexed annuity the excess interest is determined by applying a stated crediting method to a specific index or indices.

FIXED ANNUITY – A contract issued by an insurance company guaranteeing a minimum interest rate with the crediting of excess interest determined by the performance of the insurer's general account. Index annuities are fixed annuities.

FIXED DEFERRED ANNUITY – With fixed annuities, an insurance company offers a guaranteed interest rate plus safety of your principal and earnings ((subject to the claims-paying ability of the insurance company). Your interest rate will be reset periodically, based on economic and other factors, but is guaranteed to never fall below a certain rate.

FREE WITHDRAWALS – Withdrawals that are free of surrender charges.

INDEX – The underlying external benchmark upon which the crediting of excess interest is based, also a measure of the prices of a group of securities.

IRA *(INDIVIDUAL RETIREMENT ACCOUNT)* – An IRA is a tax-advantaged personal savings plan that lets an individual set aside money for retirement. All or part of the participant's contributions may be tax deductible, depending on the type of IRA chosen and the participant's personal financial circumstances. Distributions from many employer-sponsored retirement plans may be eligible to be rolled into an IRA to continue tax-deferred growth until the funds are needed. An annuity can be used as an IRA; that is, IRA funds can be used to purchase an annuity.

GLOSSARY

IRA ROLLOVER – IRA rollover is the phrase used when an individual who has a balance in an employer-sponsored retirement plan transfers that balance into an IRA. Such an exchange, when properly handled, is a tax-advantaged transaction.

LIQUIDITY – The ease with which an asset is convertible to cash. An asset with high liquidity provides flexibility, in that the owner can easily convert it to cash at any time, but it also tends to decrease profitability.

MARKET RISK – The risk of the market value of an asset fluctuating up or down over time. In a fixed or fixed indexed annuity, the original principal and credited interest are not subject to market risk. Even if the index declines, the annuity owner would receive no less than their original principal back if they decided to cash in the policy at the end of the surrender period. Unlike a security, indexed annuities guarantee the original premium and the premium is backed by, and is as safe as, the insurance company that issued it (subject to the claims-paying ability of the insurance company).

METHODOLOGY *(ALSO SEE CREDITING METHOD)* – The way that interest crediting is calculated. On fixed indexed annuities, there are a variety of different methods used to determine how index movement becomes interest credited.

MINIMUM GUARANTEED RETURN *(MINIMUM INTEREST RATE)* – Fixed indexed annuities typically provide a minimum guaranteed return over the life of the contract. At the time that the owner chooses to terminate the contract, the cash surrender value is compared to a second value calculated using the minimum guaranteed return and the higher of the two values is paid to the annuity owner.

OPTION – A contract which conveys to its holder the right, but not the obligation, to buy or sell something at a specified price on or before a given date. After this given date the option ceases to exist. Insurers typically buy options to provide for the excess interest potential. Options may be American style whereby they may be exercised at any time prior to the given date, or they may have to be exercised only during a specified window. Options that may only be exercised during a specified period are European-style options.

OPTION RISK – Most insurers create the potential for excess interest in an indexed annuity by buying options. Say that you could buy a share of stock for $50. If you bought the stock and it rose to $60 you could sell it and net a $10 profit. But, if the stock price fell to $40 you'd have a $10 loss. Instead of buying the actual stock, we could buy an option that gave us the right to buy the stock for $50 at any time over the next year. The cost of the option is $2. If the stock price rose to $60 we would exercise our option, buy the stock at $50 and make $10 (less the $2 cost of the option). If the price of the stock fell to $40, $30 or $10, we wouldn't use the option and it would expire. The loss is limited to $2—the cost of the option.

PARTICIPATION RATE – The percentage of positive index movement credited to the annuity. If the index methodology determined that the index increased 10 percent and the indexed annuity participated in 60 percent of the increase, it would be said that the contract has a 60 percent participation rate. Participation rates may also be expressed as asset fees or yield spreads.

POINT-TO-POINT – A crediting method measuring index movement from an absolute initial point to the absolute end point for a period. An index had a period starting value of 100 and a period ending value of 120. A point-to-point method would record a positive index movement of 20 [120-100] or a 20 percent positive movement [(120-100)/100]. Point-to-point usually refers to annual periods; however the phrase is also used instead of term end point to refer to multiple year periods.

PREMIUM BONUS – A premium bonus is additional money that is credited to the accumulation account of an annuity policy under certain conditions.

PUT OPTION *(ALSO SEE CALL OPTION)* – Gives the holder the right to sell an underlying security or index at a specified price on or before a given date.

QUALIFIED ANNUITIES *(QUALIFIED MONEY)* – Qualified annuities are annuities purchased for funding an IRA, 403(b) tax-deferred annuity or other type of retirement arrangements. An IRA or qualified retirement plan provides the tax deferral. An annuity contract should be used to fund an IRA or qualified retirement plan to benefit from an annuity's features other than tax deferral, including the safety features, lifetime income payout option and death benefit protection.

REQUIRED MINIMUM DISTRIBUTION *(RMD)* – The amount of money that Traditional, SEP and SIMPLE IRA owners and qualified plan participants must begin distributing from their retirement accounts by April 1 following the year they reach age 70.5. RMD amounts must then be distributed each subsequent year.

RETURN FLOOR – Another way of saying minimum guaranteed return.

ROTH IRA – Like other IRA accounts, the Roth IRA is simply a holding account that manages your stocks, bonds, annuities, mutual funds and CD's. However, future withdrawals (including earnings and interest) are typically tax-advantaged once the account has been open for five years and the account holder is age 59.5.

RULE OF 72 – Tells you approximately how many years it takes a sum to double at a given rate. It's handy to be able to figure out, without using a calculator, that when you're earning a 6 percent return, for example, by dividing 6 percent into 72, you'll find that it takes 12 years for money to double. Conversely, if you know it took a sum twelve years to double you could divide 12 into 72 to determine the annual return (6 percent).

SIMPLE INTEREST *(ALSO SEE COMPOUND INTEREST)* – Interest is only earned on the principal balance.

SPLIT ANNUITY – A split annuity is the term given to an effective strategy that utilizes two or more different annuity products—one designed to generate monthly income and the other to restore the original starting principal over a set period of time.

STANDARD & POOR'S 500 *(S&P 500)* – The most widely used external index by fixed indexed annuities. Its objective is to be a benchmark to measure and report overall U.S. stock market performance. It includes a representative sample of 500 common stocks from companies trading on the New York Stock Exchange, American Stock Exchange, and NASDAQ National Market System. The index represents the price or market value of the underlying stocks and does not include the value of reinvested dividends of the underlying stocks.

GLOSSARY

STOCK MARKET INDEX – A report created from a type of statistical measurement that shows up or down changes in a specific financial market, usually expressed as points and as a percentage, in a number of related markets, or in an economy as a whole (i.e. S&P 500 or New York Stock Exchange).

SURRENDER CHARGE – A charge imposed for withdrawing funds or terminating an annuity contract prematurely. There is no industry standard for surrender charges, that is, each annuity product has its own unique surrender charge schedule. The charge is usually expressed as a percentage of the amount withdrawn prematurely from the contract. The percentage tends to decline over time, ultimately becoming zero.

TRADITIONAL IRA – SEE IRA (INDIVIDUAL RETIREMENT ACCOUNT)

TERM END POINT – Crediting methods measuring index movements over a greater timeframe than a year or two. The opposite of an annual reset method. Also referred to as a term point-to-point method. Say that the index value was at 100 on the first day of the period. If the calculated index value was at 150 at the end of the period the positive index movement would be 50 percent (150-100/100). The company would credit a percentage of this movement as excess interest. Index movement is calculated and interest credited at the end of the term and interim movements during the period are ignored.

TERM HIGH POINT *(HIGH WATER MARK)* – A type of term end point structure that uses the highest anniversary index level as the end point. Say that the index value was at 100 on the first day of the period, reached a value of 160 at the end of a contract year during the period, and ended the period at 150. A term high

223

point method would use the 160 value—the highest contract anniversary point reached during the period, as the end point and the gross index gain would be 60 percent (160-100/100). The company would then apply a participation rate to the gain.

TERM YIELD SPREAD – A type of term end point structure which calculates the total index gain for a period, computes the annual compound rate of return deducts a yield spread from the annual rate of return and then recalculates the total index gain for the period based on the net annual rate. Say that an index increased from 100 to 200 by the end of a nine year period. This is the equivalent of an 8 percent compound annual interest rate. If the annuity had a 2 percent term yield spread this would be deducted from the annual interest rate (8 percent-2 percent) and the net rate would be credited to the contract (6 percent) for each of the nine years. Total index gain may also be computed by using the highest anniversary index level as the end point.

VARIABLE ANNUITY – A contract issued by an insurance company offering separate accounts invested in a wide variety of stocks and/or bonds. The investment risk is borne by the annuity owner. Variable annuities are considered securities and require appropriate securities registration.

1035 EXCHANGE – The 1035 exchange refers to the section of tax code that allows annuity owners the flexibility to exchange one annuity for another without incurring any immediate tax liabilities. This action is most often utilized when an annuity holder decides they want to upgrade an annuity to a more favorable one, but they do not want to activate unnecessary tax liabilities that would typically be encountered when surrendering an existing annuity contract.

401(K) ROLLOVER – SEE IRA ROLLOVER

David Tidwell

Website: www.legacyfa.net

Phone: (208) 465-0033

Email: processor@legacyfa.net

Chad Nielsen

Website: www.federalbenefitsadvice.com

Phone: (385) 229-3632 | (208) 233-4100

Email: chadn@morenow.net